William Earl Levy, Sr.
"Dean of the Fire Service"
Tallahassee Fire Chief & Family Man

William Earl Levy Sr. served in the Tallahassee Fire Department for more than 50 years, 37 of which were as Fire Chief.

©2013
Written by: Maurice Majszak
Compiled by: Maurice Majszak
Photo Courtesy of; State Archives of Florida, Florida Photographic Collection

Published by;
Southern Yellow Pine (SYP) Publishing
4351 Natural Bridge Rd.
Tallahassee, FL 32305

All Rights reserved. No part of this publication may be reproduced, stored in a retrieval system or transmitted in any form or by any means, electronic, mechanical, photocopying, recording, scanning or otherwise, without the prior written permission of the Publisher. For permission or further information contact SYP Publishing, LLC. 4351 Natural Bridge Rd. Tallahassee, FL 32305.

www.syppublishing.com

The contents and opinions expressed in this book do not necessarily reflect the views and opinions of Southern Yellow Pine Publishing, nor does the mention of brands or trade names constitute endorsement. No attempt has been made to verify facts presented by individual authors.

Copyright Maurice Majszak 2013
Front Cover photo; Courtesy of; State Archives of Florida, Florida Photographic Collection
Back Cover photo; Top - Courtesy of; State Archives of Florida, Florida Photographic Collection. Bottom – Maurice Majszak
Cover Design & Art by; Taylor Nelson
Internal Photos; Photos Courtesy of; State Archives of Florida, Florida Photographic Collection Pgs. Title Page, iii, 7, 20, 22, 33, 34, 36, 44, 53
Photo on page 35, Courtesy of Carol Albertson
Photos on pgs. 19 & 37, Courtesy of Asst. Chief Ridgway Coe

Appendix A- Permission granted from Jeanette Levy Fountain, William & Frederick Levy to publish personal and family writings.

ISBN-13: 978-0-9857062-8-9
ISBN 10 - 0985706287

Printed in the United States of America
First Edition

William Earl Levy, Sr.
"Dean of the Fire Service"
Tallahassee Fire Chief & Family Man

By: Maurice Majszak
Photo Courtesy of; State Archives of Florida, Florida Photographic Collection

Contents

Acknowledgements vii

Introduction ix

1 Early Years 1

2 Mrs. Hassell Levy 4

3 Family Life 7

4 Serving in World War II 11

5 Vacations 13

6 Christian Man of Service 15

7 Fire Department Years 18

8 Innovations 26

9 Rediscovered History 38

10 "The Chief" and "His Men" 39

11 Accomplishments 44

Appendix A Remembrances 57

- William "Bill" Levy 58

- Melba Jones – Letter to Bill Levy Regarding Hassell Levy 69

- Larry Surles – Neighbor 70

- Rick Levy – Happy Birthday Dad 73

- Rick Levy – Happy Birthday & Mother's Day 77

- Jeanette Levy Fountain 80

Appendix B ISO Classification 85

Appendix C Congressional Record and Resolutions 101

City of Tallahassee Proclamation – May 5, 1970 102

Leon County Board of Commissioners Resolution - May 4, 1970 103

State of Florida Senate Resolution – May 7, 1970 105

State of Florida Senate Resolution – April 28, 1976 106

Congressional Record — Extensions of Remarks – March 29, 1977 107

Letter from Congressman Don Fuqua to Chief Levy 109

  Florida Fire Chiefs Association – Resolution upon Chief Levy's Passing – 1986 110

Appendix D   Letters 111

- Letter from Chief Levy to Chief George McDaniel - June 30, 1971 112
- Letter from R. W. Carter to Chief Levy - August 17, 1973 113
- Letter from Delmar Publishers requesting Chief Levy write a college-level text book - January 16, 1974 114
- Letter from Ralph E. Proctor Sr. - January 28, 1975 115
- Letter from Chief Levy to Ralph E. Proctor Sr. - February 20, 1975 116
- Letter from Chief Levy to Assistant Chief Clyde Johnson - September 20, 1956 117
- Letter from Chief Levy to Deputy Chief Morris Wainwright -September 30, 1966 . 118
- Letter from Chief Levy to Deputy Chief James Cureton - March 31, 1977 119
- Letter from Chief Levy to Captain Fred Mitchell - August 15, 1975 120
- Retirement Request from Chief Levy to City Manager, Daniel A. Kleman - November 30, 1977 121
- Letter from Chief Levy to Maryland State Fire Marshal, James C. Robertson – March 9, 1979 123
- Letter from City Manager, Daniel A. Kleman to Chief Levy - September 28, 1978 125

Appendix E   Miscellaneous Documents 127

- Training Syllabus 128
- Chief Levy on Fire Prevention December 8, 1945 – *Tallahassee Democrat* 130
- City publication *Panarama of Progress* – April, 1966 131
- "Good Government" newspaper article – *Tallahassee Democrat* 133
- "How to Protect You from Fire" *Memphis Press-Scimitar* February 21, 1957 134
- Letter from Chief Levy to Mrs. J. Kittrell on the history of the old fire bell – February 27, 1975 135

Acknowledgements

Chief Mack Flowers (Retired), of the Avon Park Fire Department, edited an article on Chief Levy by Charlie Deal that appeared in the Aug. 1986 edition of *Florida Fireman*. Information from that article was used throughout this manuscript. I thought it only fitting that the Editor's Note from Chief Flowers' article be included, without change.

> "Editor's note: Chief Levy was my favorite Fire Chief and idol. I had many interesting and pleasant conversations during my brief friendship with him. I learned much from this man and was always pleased to hear him call me "Brother Mack." He will be sorely missed by me and all other people associated with the fire service. On behalf of myself and the Florida State Firemen's Association, we extend our deepest sympathy to his family. It is God's gain and our loss."

A special thanks to the following individuals for their assistance in writing this manuscript:

- Assistant Chief Ridgway Coe (Retired) - Who willingly shared his personal knowledge of Chief Levy with the author.
- Robbie Robertson, Maryland State Fire Marshal (Retired) - For initial review of this narrative and helpful suggestions.
- Mike Knowles, Tallahassee firefighter - Who served under Chief Levy and shared his experiences.
- Jeanette Levy Fountain, sister - For providing family input, which has been included in this manuscript.
- Bill Levy, son - Who shared information regarding their home and family life. Bill was also very helpful in editing this manuscript. His

suggestions and comments, for the most part, have been included in this manuscript.
- Rick Levy, son - Who shared information regarding their home and family life.
- Larry Surles – Chief Levy's neighbor.
- To all the members of the Tallahassee Fire Department, current and retired, who shared their stories and made this manuscript as accurate as possible.

Introduction

The Tallahassee Fire Department hired me as the Senior Fire Plans Examiner on December 19, 2005. I have always been interested in history, in particular the Civil War and World War II. My military experience as a crypto-linguist trained me to take bits and pieces of seemingly unrelated information and put them together to see the complete picture. Shortly after being hired, I became interested in the history of the Tallahassee Fire Department because of the abundance of information that was available and the stories that were told about the old firefighters.

Enthused by all the information that was available and the opportunity to meet and talk with active and retired firefighters, it did not take long for me to decide to write a book on the history of the department. The book *Remembering the Tallahassee Fire Department* is a pictorial history of the department, with related information included, and was published in early 2012.

My interest in documenting the history of the department was well-known. One day while passing by a deputy chief's office, he offered me a file folder about ½" thick and said that if I did not want it, it was going to be thrown in the trash. I accepted the folder, not knowing what was in it, since I did not want fire history to be thrown away. As it turned out, the folder contained the personnel file of Fire Chief William "Earl" Levy, Sr.

Looking through the file I noted how much and how well his professional life was documented and started writing notes on the information I found. I soon realized that the facts were being organized and there was enough information to write a book on Chief Levy's professional life.

I had met both William "Bill" and Frederick "Rick" Levy, the Chief's sons when they purchased my first book. I contacted Bill and asked if the family would like to review my manuscript prior to being published. They answered in the affirmative. During this process, Bill informed me that he and Rick had previously written things about their dad, as had Jeanette Fountain (Levy's sister) just to document the Chief's life. They gave me copies of what they had written, with permission to use whatever I wanted in the book. Bill also gave me a copy of remembrances that were written by his childhood friend and neighbor, Larry Surles.

After reading what the family members had written, I knew that my book on Chief Levy would be about both his personal life as a husband and father, and his professional life as "Dean of the Fire Service."

1

Early Years

Chief Levy came from a very close, working-class, Christian family. He was born in the family home in Tallahassee, Florida on November 16, 1910, to Fred and Bessie Levy. He had two younger sisters, Jeanette and Myrtle, and an older brother, O'Neal.

"How about getting a baby sister when you are 25 years old and married? Earl did!" recalled Jeanette. "Our mother had three brothers and four sisters. Our mother gave birth to her two boys at the same time as our grandmother had her last two children – boys! Imagine the fun and camaraderie and love each of these eleven first cousins had. They all lived close enough to walk to each other's home. Eating, sleeping, playing and praying were all shared activities! They were just like brothers!" (J. Fountain[1])

Levy had many cousins that he played with growing up. His mother, Bessie Adele Atkinson Levy, had three sisters and three brothers, all of whom raised their children in the Tallahassee area. Bessie's sister, Maude, married Thomas Pinkney "TP" Coe, who joined the Tallahassee Volunteer Fire Company in 1906. Coe was appointed Fire Chief on July 12, 1912 and served in that capacity until April 30, 1940, when he resigned. His nephew, Earl, was then appointed as Chief to what had become the Tallahassee Fire Department.

Levy was immersed in the fire service from a young age. Both his father and uncle, Eugene, were members of the Tallahassee Volunteer Fire Company in

---

[1] See Appendix A for other remembrances by Jeanette Levy Fountain (pg. 80)

the early 1900s. Although it is unknown how long the two volunteered, Fred Levy was involved in the taxi business, operating cars for hire in the early 1920s.

One of Levy's friends and playmate was Leroy Collins, who later served as Governor of Florida in the mid-1950s.[2] O'Neal and Leroy Collins were both born in the same year, grew up together and remained close friends throughout their lives. Complications during delivery at O'Neal's birth left him with uncontrollable twitches; however, his mental capabilities were not affected. Other children liked to make fun of him. Younger brother Earl, however, was quick to defend him, and became known as somewhat of a fighter. If you messed with O'Neal, you were messing with Earl!

"My dad, Earl Levy, grew up defending and protecting a family member who had health problems, and he also helped members of my mother's family. Throughout his life he continued to help those who needed assistance – friends, relatives, employees and even strangers." (B. Levy[3])

Caring for his brother gave Levy a deep compassion for all, especially those less fortunate than him. On occasion, O'Neal would eat at a restaurant or go to the drug store for candy and forget to pay. Every Monday the merchants would go to the fire station and present the bills to the Chief, who would settle his brother's accounts.

---

[2] Leroy Collins served as Governor of Florida from January 4, 1955 to January 3, 1961.

[3] See Appendix A for other remembrances by Bill Levy (pg. 58)

"Kids today want cell phones and electronic games, but Dad said that during his younger years, instant status was obtained by a boy who had a wagon, and a Billy goat to pull it. Those rigs were scarce in his neighborhood, but he and his friends did not lack for fun, adventure, and competition. They built and flew kites, and made tractors and whirligigs from items commonly available around the house. They drew circles in the dirt, and played marbles "for keeps." They spun their homemade tops in similar circles, and in those days of winners and losers, many tops changed hands after being knocked out of the ring by a competitor."

"Almost every boy had a pocket knife, which they used daily, sometimes to play versions of mumblety peg, where two opponents stand facing each other and alternate throwing their knives to stick in the ground. Each must move his foot to parallel where the opponent's knife landed. The object is to make the other guy place his feet so close together that he chickens out, or spread your opponent's feet until he can't stretch far enough to reach the knife. The knives were also essential in making popguns that shot chinaberries hard enough to raise a welt, and the popguns were used in games that allowed the boys to experience being on both the giving and receiving end." (B. Levy)

Levy's early schooling took place under the watchful eye of one of Leon County's premier educators, the legendary Kate Sullivan. "In addition to being an outstanding teacher, Dad said that she was able to maintain discipline without even raising her voice; approaching any student who was being disruptive, and peering at them sternly over her glasses. That look reminded them that stronger measures could soon follow, and was usually sufficient to make students settle down on the spot." (B. Levy) Levy finished two years at Leon High School before joining the Tallahassee Volunteer Fire Company at age 16 as a paid driver.

2

Mrs. Hassell Levy

As a young man of 20 years old, Levy courted Hassell Williams of Savannah, Georgia, and then married her on December 28, 1931. But before he met his future wife, the young fireman had a few adventures in dating. Bill Levy told me one story in particular.

Before Levy met Hassell, he dated a girl who lived in Calvary, Ga. Several local boys showed their discontent by chasing him one night as he left town and headed towards Tallahassee. He opened up a big lead on them, but his engine started skipping, the car slowed, and he wondered if he would get home in one piece. He glanced in the rear view mirror just as a big hog ran across the road behind him. The car, full of Georgia boys, hit the hog, and continued on into a ditch.

As the story goes, Levy did not go back to check on them. He did stop just long enough to tap on the carburetor with a wrench to free the sticking float before resuming his trip home. Bill told me, the close call didn't keep his dad from dating attractive Georgia girls. Hassell was born in Rome, Ga. They met after she had moved to Tallahassee. That was probably better than him leaving town for a date, and hoping for more divine intervention if he needed it.

Chief Levy often said that Hassell was the best wife a man could have. Hassell came from a Christian family. She was living a modest but happy life in Pooler, Georgia, when her mother died. Her life changed drastically. Bill Levy quoted his mother as saying; "When the seventh child, Roland Morrison, was born, Mother took pneumonia and died. We were stunned and in shock for years. I was almost 12. Imagine a man being left with seven children all under fifteen years of age and one of them an infant, suddenly losing his wife. I tell you, Daddy did a lot of praying."

Hassell was born in Rome, Georgia, on May 9, 1911, and passed in Tallahassee, Florida on August 18, 2000. She rests next to Earl in Oakland Cemetery, Tallahassee.

At age 18, Hassell and her sister Eloise moved from Pooler, Georgia to Tallahassee. Hassell was hired by the local telephone company as a switchboard operator, and was then promoted to chief operator a year later, where she was responsible for hiring, firing and training. Later, while her children were in school, she continued to work part time as a PBX switchboard operator at the First National Bank. She retired from the bank with more than 20 years of service.

Melba Jones, Chief Levy's secretary for 20 years, recalled how the Chief met Hassell. She said, "He met two girls while walking down Monroe Street one morning on an errand for Chief T.P. Coe. One girl was an acquaintance, and she introduced them. Levy said that he decided right then and there that she was the prettiest girl he had ever seen. He ended by saying, "and you know something, I still think she is the prettiest girl I've ever seen! She was more than pretty, she was a wonderful person."[4]

After that first meeting, Earl knew he wanted to date Hassell, but she wouldn't go out with him since he had been dating one of her best friends. After Hassell's friend gave her blessing they started dating, and neither one ever went out with anyone else.

---

[4] See Appendix A for Mrs. Melba Jones' letter to Bill Levy (pg. 69)

Earl married Hassell; he accepted and supported her family as his. Chief Levy raised and provided for his wife's two younger sisters and served as a father figure for his niece and nephew (Hassell's sister's children). In addition to the profound, gentle lessons about life she imparted to her own two sons and her grandchildren, Hassell taught first graders in Sunday School at First Baptist Church for more than 30 years, where she influenced the lives of literally hundreds. (B. Levy)

Levy, Earl W., Stout, Arthur., Adkinson, Ira., Stout, George. Photo Courtesy of; State Archives of Florida, Florida Photographic Collection

3

Family Life

Earl and Hassell bought several lots in a corner of E. 8th Avenue, what was then a cow pasture, on the site of the ring tournaments held in Tallahassee, 1850-1870. Ring tournaments derived from the sport of jousting. Rather than trying to knock another rider down, as in jousting, a ring tournament participant negotiated a course ranging between 80 and 125 feet long on horseback, attempting to spear a series of small (1/2" - to 2") rings suspended overhead using an 8½-foot lance. Whoever speared the most rings was the winner. The couple designed a house, and in the early 1940s it was built by Mr. Middlebrooks at 534 E. 8th Ave. The house was one of the first in the area, and just within the city limits. Levy loved to ride horses, and they soon built a barn on part of their property adjacent to the house, but located in the county.

Hassell had never been on a horse, but learned to ride after she and Earl got married, in order to spend more time with her husband. At age 82, Hassell took a "Writing for Fun" class, and had this to say about those days: "When Earl and I had a place to keep horses, he bought a huge gray gaited horse named Eagle for himself, and a mare for me. I named her Scarlette because of her beautiful red coat. She was gentle, and just my size. Her mother died at her birth so she had to be raised on a bottle, which accounted for her small size.

I amazed myself by even mounting a horse, as I had never been around horses and they alarmed me, but Earl bought me some riding boots and brown jodhpurs and I looked the part, so I had to try. I found I really enjoyed it, and even rode Eagle a time or two. It was therapy for Earl, and he rode almost every afternoon, many times alone.

Earl and other horse lovers formed, what they named, the Trot-a-Way Club and we had so many marvelous morning rides, ending at a pond to cook breakfast. Also late afternoon rides ending with supper. We held several horse shows in Tallahassee out on the Old St. Augustine Road at the Tacot Stables."

Bill Levy remembers spending time with the horses, as well. But, like so many good memories, they finally came to an end. "When the property used for the horse lot was eventually annexed into the city, Dad boarded the horses with a man who owned lakefront property on Lake Jackson. We went there to see the horses several times, but as I recall, Dad never rode either one of them again."

Levy enlisted and served in the Army for a short time during WWII. His wife recalled things changing quite a lot soon after he came back to Tallahassee. "After Earl returned from Ft. Bliss where he was stationed, our first baby was born and my riding days were over." Levy returned home on June 10, 1945, and their family began to grow. To Earl and Hassell Levy two sons were born, William Earl, Jr., and Fredrick Cartwright. His children and their families were the pride of his life.

One story about Levy and his keen people-sense and consummate kindness remains vivid in his son Bill's memory. "At about age 11, I had been riding a vintage conventional bicycle we found at Grandmother's house; it was well-used even before I got it. After I added many a mile, I began to think maybe I was ready to move up to an "English Bike" with gears, but Dad was not sure I could handle such a high performance machine, and talked about having my bike re-conditioned."

"A friend and I each asked Santa for a new bicycle, and with all the confidence of youth we made a pact to meet and go for a nice long ride after Christmas. When I mentioned this plan to Dad, he asked that I tell him some more about my friend. I described him as best I could, and concluded by saying that he was nice and I liked him a lot. Dad asked specifically where my friend lived, and we drove by the house and yard. Dad said not a word; he saw the same things that I did, but understood a lot more."

"I woke up Christmas morning, scrambled out of bed, and ran hopefully towards the living room. Leaning on the kickstand and ready to go was a beautiful "English bike."

"But there is more to the story. In the days prior to Christmas, Dad had my conventional bike painted and re-conditioned with a new chain and tires. On Christmas day he told me that if my friend didn't get a bike for Christmas, I should offer to let him use it whenever he wanted to, and that is the way things developed."

"We had a fireplace in our living room, and I recall many a cold morning when Dad built a roaring fire before I had even gotten out of bed. If he went outside for more firewood, I would often hear the ring of the ax as he cut the wood to size. He finally installed a gas log in the fireplace, but kept the owl-shaped andirons. The owls will always remind me of warm wood fires on cold mornings, and coals that flickered as our family relaxed in the living room after supper. Many years later, they now reside in my oldest daughter's house, but they still bring back memories from my childhood."

As can be read in Bill Levy's "Remembrances" in Appendix A, many of the memories he has of his father involve the outdoors. "We also hunted squirrels in the river swamp, including the area just off the Old Plank Road near Newport. Dad told me that when he was a young boy, his whole family often packed a lunch and drove to the nearby sulfur spring pool, for a day of relaxing and swimming in the ice cold water. Mom and I took a lunch and swam there with relatives several times."

"Dad loved to fish. When I was still a young boy he taught me to silently paddle a boat on area lakes. He later taught me how to row and control a boat in the swift current of the St. Marks River. My oldest daughter, Cyndi, now has the oars that we used displayed on a wall in her house. He showed me how to slingshot a cricket up under a low hanging limb when fishing with a cane pole, how to use a bait casting reel, and how to place a plug or plastic worm just where I wanted to put it."

Rick remembers his dad always being there. "Football games, basketball games, track meets, PTA meetings, band concerts, singing events … How many hours (hundreds of hours)…?"(R. Levy[5]) He knew his dad and mom were there, and tried that much harder because he knew they were watching.

"Although his job was very stressful, Dad didn't let it get the best of him, and I don't recall him ever being cross or irritable at home or around our family. I especially remember him singing in the car when our family took trips. (Years later as a supervisor, I understood how having outstanding employees could put someone in more of a singing mood.) Mom and Dad were both most comfortable singing informally, but I don't think they gave themselves enough credit. Mom played the piano well, and they both had good voices. When I was quite young, they would each periodically sing portions of popular songs such as "When Irish Eyes Are Smiling", "Bonnie Banks o'Loch Lomond", "You Take the High Road", etc. They were both happy when they sang, or perhaps they sang because they were happy." (B. Levy)

In a letter to his father on the occasion of his 70th birthday, Rick summed up the character of Earl Levy as a family man. "You have been a father. No, not just "fathered" us; been a father to us. You have cared about our needs, and have been there to meet them. You've taught us what it means to be a husband, a father, a man."

_____

[5] See Appendix A for Happy Birthday letter by Rick Levy (pg. 73)

4

Serving in World War II

Jeanette Fountain, Levy's sister, recalls what it was like watching her much-older brother enlist in the Army and go fight for his country. "World War II years in Tallahassee (I was six years old) brought about loyalty and true patriotism everywhere. Those eligible volunteered (including our cousins). Earl was told that he wasn't eligible (to serve in the Army) because of the ruling that administrators of life-saving agencies must remain "in place". Did I mention the Levy hard-headedness? Earl organized a plan, including an interim chief, and motored to Jacksonville to enlist in the U.S. Army. My mother cried for many days thereafter, but he had made his decision. To this day, I believe it was the right one for him."

Chief Levy received basic training at Ft. Bliss, Texas and remained there, having been assigned to the station complement, post office section. While at Fort Bliss, he attended the Field Lineman course of training. During Levy's absence from the fire department, Lieutenant George L. McDaniel, the main character in the scheme that enabled him to enlist, was promoted to Acting Fire Chief. Levy served for 8 ½ months, receiving an Honorable discharge on June 10, 1945. Chief Levy resumed his duties in Tallahassee on Monday, June 11, 1945. The Chief thought so very highly of McDaniel that upon his retirement, Chief Levy sent him a letter making him an honorary life-time Assistant Chief.[6]

Shortly after his service in the Army, in the middle 1940s, Levy contracted rheumatic fever, which incapacitated him for many months. Fortunately he overcame it. "I was very young when Dad was confined to bed with rheumatic fever, and Assistant Chief Morris Wainwright came by the house often to visit

---

[6] See Appendix D for complete letter (pg. 112)

with Dad, and discuss fire department business. Mom usually asked me to find out if they wanted "hot tea or cold tea" to drink, and I ran through the house as fast as I could to get their orders and deliver them back to her in the kitchen. By the time Dad fully recovered and returned to work, he and Morris Wainwright had consumed gallons of tea together.   Chief Wainwright was not a timid man, but only then did he confess to Mom that while in the Navy he became a confirmed coffee drinker, and really didn't care much for tea, be it hot or cold. Mom was quite surprised, and said that she would have gladly made coffee if he had only spoken up. At that point, I understand that both of them managed to find some humor in the situation." (B. Levy)

5

Vacations

According to Hassell Levy correspondence dated March 1, 1977, "Every year Earl attended the Florida, Southeastern, or International Fire Chief meetings, and (on the way) we got to at least pass through every state except Alaska and Hawaii. Earl always took his vacation at that time so we could take the children with us, and we made the trips as educational as possible."

"When we went to Los Angeles we took nine days driving out, and made side trips to all the places of interest on the way. The International meetings were always held in September, so we had to get permission from teachers in order to take the kids out of school. Most said that they would learn more than they would learn in school in the same length of time, although Bill's algebra teacher and his football coach would have been happy for him to stay home, as we were going to be gone three weeks."

"We made the trips with the Lakeland Fire Chief Charlie Deal and his wife after that, and enjoyed their company for 25 years or more. After Earl and Charlie retired they decided to make a trip out West instead of going to the meeting. It was the best trip we ever made. They decided every night where they wanted to go the next day. We went all the way to Canada and Long View, Washington."

There was a little bit of a different view from the backseat, however. "Chief Deal and his wife drove from Lakeland, and caravanned with Dad and our family to a week-long International Fire Chief's convention in Los Angeles, California. Mom's sister Eloise sat between me and Rick in the back seat of our '58 Chevy, to lessen the chance we would get on Dad's nerves. Dad drove all the way out and back (which probably consumed two weeks, round trip), and

Rick and I got our first exposure to Route 66, mountain driving, traffic on the LA Freeway and smog." (B. Levy)

"After the convention, visiting Hoover Dam, the Painted Desert, Meteor Crater, the Grand Canyon, and other historic or scenic sights was quite educational for all of us. I don't doubt that Dad was glad to get back to the relative peace and quiet of life in Tallahassee, after driving over 5,000 miles with two young boys in the back seat." (B. Levy)

Upon their return from one such trip, someone asked Chief Levy what was the best thing that he saw on the trip. Retired firefighter Don Pumphrey recalls his chief's response: "The sign up on Thomasville Road that says Tallahassee."

6

Christian Man of Service

No story on Chief William Earl Levy, Sr. would be complete without ensuring that the readers comprehend Chief Levy's deep religious convictions. Every day of his life he reveled in the Baptist faith and music.

He was a men's Sunday School teacher and deacon at the First Baptist Church in Tallahassee for many years. He also served as chaplain for the Florida Fire Chiefs Association for a number of years. Religion was always first with Chief Levy. This is very evident when you read his answers to a questionnaire he filled out for the Cooper-Taylor Award in 1957. It is worth repeating his answer to question #1:

    Question: What do you consider important in life and most worth working towards?

    Answer: My firm belief in God is the most important thing to me. Within this personal conviction lies the belief that every Christian should develop his life to its fullest potential. My life's work has centered around fire protection. My motivation was in this direction, personally and through other people.

Chief Levy loved God through Jesus Christ. He was a prayerful man and often taught men's bible school classes, even traveling out of town to teach others the word of the Lord. According to his sister, Jeanette, Earl's one desire was to be the kind of man who was a good enough role model to not let his brother stumble. He said to his mother many times that the Lord kept this, loudly and clearly, as a motto for Earl Levy.

"'Good neighbor' describes Chief Levy. He was also a Christian in the best sense of the word. By example, manner and a calm and humorous attitude, Mr. Levy always served as a model for me. He never spoke ill of anyone, never made an off-color remark or expressed anger inappropriately. Yet, he told the funniest stories and seemed to enjoy life way beyond most people. Young boys sometimes venture into projects or get into mischief when they should not. When Bill and I did so, Mr. Levy was firm in his correction, but even-tempered and calm, no matter the transgression." (Larry Surles[7])

"Chief Levy took the time to make sure young boys were occupied with wholesome endeavors. He helped us construct a basketball goal behind the house. He took us out to target practice with our .22s or to hunt squirrels, while teaching us gun handling, safety, and responsibility. I would never have been able to learn such things without him. Mr. Levy let us have fun, too. He allowed us to be boys, but made sure we understood the boundaries of good behavior. Even after I was a grown man, Mr. Levy would stop me on the street, say "hello", and ask about Mom and the family." (Larry Surles)

"I will always remember his kindness and support when my Dad died unexpectedly. The family, especially Mom, was devastated by the suddenness of the event. Mr. Levy, like a good "Chief", was first on the scene; with words of comfort and caring for my mom, and prayer for my dad. During that time of grief, I was consoled by Mr. Levy's presence and quiet support. He went beyond expectations, driving 120 miles round trip several times to Madison, Florida to be with the family at the funeral home and to attend services. Mr. Levy also attended my dad's interment. I was almost numb from grief, but Mr. Levy's firm handshake and comforting words helped me get through the day. That's the person he was – always there when you needed him." (Larry Surles).

---

[7] See Appendix A for the Remembrance by Larry Surles (pg. 70)

Chief Robertson, formerly fire marshal for the state of Maryland, also served in the Gainesville, Alachua County area. He recalls that Chief Levy stayed at the Robertson house when in town to address the local Fellowship of Christian Firefighters.

Chief Levy visited the sick and needy while contributing more than a fair share in every way. In 1964, when firefighter, Jimmy Calloway, (8-28-1961/2-14-1964) resigned from the fire department, it was to devote more time to church activities and his family. He wrote to Levy, "It is a privilege to work for a Christian man such as yourself."

In 1951, a fireman not yet vested in the retirement system was injured and unable to work. When he returned to the station, he was evaluated for five months until Chief Levy was positive that the man would never recover sufficiently to fully perform firefighting duties. Levy and City Manager Dan Kleman supported the man by approving three months' severance pay, and the Tallahassee Fire Department sent an additional $252 to help pay his outstanding Orlando hospital bill. As a Christian, Levy wanted to help relieve the financial concerns for the man and his family, yet spare them embarrassment. He requested that the family be immediately notified of the contribution, but that the source of the funds only be identified as an anonymous charitable donation.

7

Fire Department Years

Earl Levy was employed by the Tallahassee Fire Department March 15, 1927 at age 16 and stayed to work for more than 50 years as a fireman and 37 years as Chief of the department. Levy never intended to be a fireman for very long, when he first became a driver for the Volunteer Fire Company. He wasn't sure then what he might want to do with his life. But the man who would one day lead the Tallahassee Fire Department to unparalleled accomplishments, found out soon enough what he was meant to do with his life.

His first emergency response, at age 16, taught him that fire could not only destroy property, but could take the lives of citizens. An article on Levy in the April 10, 1974 issue of the *Tallahassee Gazette,* described the gruesome scene: "…got a call to come to the old Studebaker place on Calhoun Street, where a mechanic had tipped over a can of gasoline while working under a car and dowsed himself with liquid flame. As the man ran screaming from the garage, his body was already a fatal inferno, a sixteen-year-old boy watched helplessly as the victim's life melted away… From that moment, the boy with the look and build of a man, has known just what it means to be a fireman." In Levy's own words, "I really hadn't intended it as a career at first but it only took a little while to get convinced. Once it gets in a person's blood, he is a fireman for life. I guess that's me."

Experience gained through progressive responsibility taught him the dangers of firefighting, and how quickly fire could also affect the health and lives of his men. Strong opinions about how things should be done came from years of observation, and input from others. He knew that safe and effective firefighting required capable, dedicated and well trained personnel, state-of-the-art equipment, teamwork, maximum effort, and constant attention to detail. His expectations were high, but the safety record of the department and outstanding insurance rating achieved by the city are indications that those expectations were met.

Earl's uncle, Thomas Pinkney "T.P." Coe, was fire chief when fireman Levy was hired by the city. Shortly after Levy began working with the department, Chief Coe attended the first conference of the Southeastern Fire Chiefs Association in Atlanta, Georgia. The theme for the conference was "Improving the Fire Service through Training and Education." Coe was affected by what he learned. Realizing his limitations and age, upon his return he looked within the department for a dependable person to develop as a training officer, and selected fireman Levy. Coe supported Levy and began sending him to various venues where fire service training was being conducted. As a result, Levy became one of the best informed persons in the country regarding fire equipment, fire training, fire service issues, and fire department management. Coe and Levy remained very close friends throughout their lives.

Fireman Earl Levy (*left*), Fire Chief T.P. Coe, 1940
Photo courtesy of Assistant Chief Ridgway Coe (Retired)

In the 1974 *Tallahassee Gazette* article, Chief Levy had this to say about the way things were when he was first hired: "In those days there were no child labor laws; the only requirement was that you be physically big enough to do the work." He was young for the job and started as a paid driver but there was never any question that he was equal to the task. "It's true I was young but in those days, things were different. People grew up faster. I was brought up when a dime was a dime, and you had to absolutely scratch as hard as you could for as long as you could. In those days when the department had very little money for equipment firefighting was a rough business."

Fire Chief T.P. Coe resigned on April 30, 1940, and then served as the City Fire Inspector until his death in 1948. On May 1, 1940, at age 29, fireman William "Earl" Levy, Sr. was appointed Chief of the Tallahassee Fire Department. When he took over as Chief, the fire department had nine men and one station that served a community of about 12,000 people. When he retired at age 67 in 1978, the fire department had seven engine companies, two ladder units and 125 firemen. As of this writing (May, 2013), the Tallahassee Fire Department has personnel numbering approximately 260 and 15 stations throughout Leon County.

Chief Levy at Chief Coe's Retirement – Shaking hands, 1940
Photo Courtesy of; State Archives of Florida, Florida Photographic Collection

Back then the Tallahassee Fire Department had only two trucks, and they had to cover a lot of ground. The danger of fire was great and ever present. "The biggest fire hazard at that time, were those wood-shingled roofs that covered most of the buildings in town. One spark from a coal or cinder would have set a building on fire in nothing flat," said Chief Levy. The second problem was the possibility of a "conflagration" (a chain reaction effect) that had the potential of destroying an entire section of the city if not brought quickly under control. Levy stated, "Any shower of sparks from one burning building could ignite another structure two or three blocks away, and without the manpower to patrol the vicinity, the whole thing could get out of hand."

The largest conflagration in Tallahassee was before Earl Levy was born. On May 5, 1843 about 5:00 P.M., a fire started in the kitchen of Washington Hall Hotel on Monroe and Madison. It burned most of the business district in about 3 hours when it ran out of fuel (wood) to burn. The fire was bounded by Madison Street on the South, Park Avenue on the North, Calhoun Street on the East, and Adams Street on the West. The wide empty area on Park Avenue, and a shift in wind direction, caused the fire to go back to where it had already burned everything. This kept the fire from continuing.

Chief Levy never experienced a conflagration but on December 1, 1967, Mendelson's Department Store located at 111 S. Monroe Street, caught fire and burned for two days. Levy stated, "It took us hours, and they seemed like days, before we finally got that one under control." It was wedged into a tight section of buildings on the 100-block of South Monroe Street, next door to Leon Federal Credit Union. It was the worst fire since 1843 in terms of property loss, with more than $1 million in property and goods damaged. Captain W.O. Kinard was the only firefighter injured on the fire scene. He received steam burns to the eyes, received treatment, and returned to work within hours. Levy was quoted as saying, "That was the most difficult fire I ever faced, the building was totally involved and it was jammed between several other buildings that could have easily ignited as well." According to retired Assistant Chief

Ridgway Coe, the fire traveled through the basement area where firewalls had been breached. Fire wall doors could not be closed due to obstructions.

Firemen are shown protecting the David Walker Library. Smoke is coming out of Mendelson's Department Store and hose streams are directed to keep the fire from impinging on the historic Walker Library.
Photo Courtesy of; State Archives of Florida, Florida Photographic Collection

The David Walker Library, at 209 E. Park Avenue, was one of the most treasured structures in Tallahassee, with countless irreplaceable manuscripts and out-of-print books. It was endangered by that fire in 1967. Fire blackened bricks are still visible today on the south side of the library. Firemen with hose streams were placed on the roof of the adjacent building to the west, and in the nearby alley to contain the fire and keep it from spreading to the library and destroying its valuable contents.

"Like the rest of the fire department vehicles, Dad's red Chief's car had a two-way radio and a siren. He parked it in front of our house when he was home, and one day at about age four, I got the bright idea of very quietly trying the siren out myself. I gently bumped the foot switch, and was pleased that the resulting low moan was not too loud. But the sound persisted for so long that I was afraid Dad would hear it. Pushing on the siren brake button would have stopped it from spinning, but I was a bit too scared to experiment further, and decided to see what could be done from outside the car. Fortunately, nobody heard the whirling siren but me, and it had slowed down enough that I wasn't seriously hurt when I stuck my finger in it." (B. Levy)

Bill's personal curiosity for all things fire department didn't stop at the siren. "Dad's personal car was parked in the driveway when not in use, and was also equipped with a two-way radio. I had often been with him when he was paged and took the microphone from its holder on the dash and responded."

"One day I got in the car by myself and turned on the radio to monitor the traffic. Things must have been a bit slow, since it was not long before I picked up the microphone. I was pretty proud of myself for remembering his call sign and said "Calling Car 14. Calling Car 14, come in", which was what I heard when we were in his city car and someone was trying to reach him; I vaguely wondered why he did not respond."

"I was happy to see him drive up soon thereafter, and was so young and naïve that I wondered why he didn't seem happy to see me too. When he asked why I had been on the fire department radio, I didn't even understand how he knew about it. I don't remember getting a whipping; I remember the crime, but not the punishment. But I am sure I got a good talking to, and I got the message."

"Dad also had a radio monitor at home. When an alarm came in at night he listened for the location and nature of the fire, and evaluated the potential for property damage and danger to his men. Depending on what he learned from radio traffic or concluded on his own, he would either contact the station for more information, dress immediately and go to the scene of the fire, or go back to bed." (B. Levy)

Because Chief Levy left such a legacy of strength, professionalism and service, it is no surprise that there are quite a few stories revolving around him that have trickled down through the years in the fire department. Stories like these are what turn an incredible man into a legend.

When Chief Levy had a spare moment at the main station, one of his favorite pastimes was arm wrestling. Levy was a big man with broad shoulders and was very strong. Nobody beat Chief Levy at arm wrestling, not even Joe Vinzant; he would beat Joe every time.

Assistant Chief Joe Vinzant was extremely strong, and could climb the fire pole in the station using only his hands. He was one of only a couple of firefighters who could start the American LaFrance fire engines by using the hand crank at the front, and he once picked up a fire truck by himself. He would back up to a rear wheel of the Number 1 pumper at the main station, grab two of the wooden spokes, and pick the tire and truck completely up off the concrete floor.

At one fire, Chief Levy went into the burning building and found the nozzle man. He grabbed the firefighter's collar by one hand and when the Chief wanted the hose stream to be moved, he lifted the fireman off the ground and turned the fireman and hose to where he wanted the water delivered.

Chief Levy did not get upset very easily, however, in 1966 a new probationary firefighter was assigned to clean up the dormitory area of the main station at 109 S. Adams-Street. He played a payback prank on another fireman and glued what he thought was the other man's locker shut. The latter had previously, jokingly, gotten some glue on the probationary fireman's shirt. Since his shirt was wrecked, he thought that a payback was in order. Shirts were expensive and hard to come by back then.

The probationary firefighter was swabbing the floor when Chief Levy came in and tried to open his own locker, but couldn't because it was glued shut. Levy must have thought that his locker had been targeted, because he said "I can't believe there is anyone in our organization who would do that; he is dealing with something deadlier than a Nazi gallows," and promised to fire the person who did it (B. Levy). The wood cracked before the locker ever opened, and the culprit was never found; one retired firefighter said that it was the best kept secret in the department.

The secret of who glued the Chief's locker shut bugged Deputy Chief Raymond Love (Jan. 29, 1954 – Jan. 31, 1985) to no end. After he retired he still tried to find out who did it. On a Sunday afternoon a couple of weeks before Love passed, several retired firefighters including Lt. Jimmy Byrd (May 1, 1969 – Dec. 31, 1996, Retired), went to his house. The guilty firefighter confessed because he knew that Love had always wanted to know who did the dastardly deed. The fire service is truly a brotherhood of firefighters, and the foregoing also shows how much these firemen, who lived and worked together for years, respected and loved one another long after their firefighting days.

8

Innovations

The "Insurance Service Office" (ISO) assigns classifications which are used for determining a city's overall insurance premiums; the lower the ISO classification, the lower a community's insurance rates.

Chief Levy realized the importance of a low ISO Classification and strived to ensure that the citizens of Tallahassee had the lowest ISO Classification possible. Under his guidance, the City of Tallahassee's fire insurance classification was successively lowered from a Class 6 on May 6, 1940, to a Class 2 in 1973.

While a Class 1 rating has never been achieved in Tallahassee, a Class 2 rating could be attained by accumulating 1000 points or less out of 5000, and in 1973, the Tallahassee Fire Department's Class 2 rating resulted from receiving 916 points. There were no Class 1 cities in the South and only about 30 cities throughout the country with a Class 2 rating. Three of the 30 cities – Tallahassee, Memphis and Baton Rouge – were in the south. The entire 1973 report, which details the water supply, fire department, fire service communication and fire safety controls, is reproduced in Appendix B[8]. The report gives the reader a good knowledge base as to the capabilities of the Tallahassee Fire Department in that era, as well as what the ISO looked for in classifying a city's rating.

Regarding the ISO rating, Levy stated in the April 10, 1974 issue of the *Tallahassee Gazette*, "This kind of success is a group effort. It requires two things: a good fire department and good water facilities. That means full

---

[8] See Appendix B page 85.

cooperation from all city departments, and that's what we have in Tallahassee." Chief Levy relayed his feelings to the entire fire department on November 28, 1973. He had the following memorandum posted at all stations:

"To All Fire Department Personnel:

I am sure all of you know by now that our city has been placed in a Class 2 category on the ISO grading schedule.

This achievement is the end result of many long years of dedicated fire protection service to the citizens of Tallahassee.

It is my purpose in this communication to point out that our status today is the result of an <u>overall team effort.</u> There is not one of you who has not contributed towards this effort and many of you to a degree far beyond the ordinary call of duty.

As your Chief, I wish to express to all of you my most heartfelt congratulations and personal gratitude for such a fine outstanding group of men <u>without which</u> our goal would have <u>never</u> been achieved.

Earl Levy

Chief, Fire Department"

Chief Levy was not afraid to try new equipment or methods. Many fire service improvements and innovations that are credited to someone else were first developed or tested by personnel of the Tallahassee Fire Department. Some of the innovations, as recollected by others, are as follows:

a. The first jaws-of-life were pressurized by a hydraulic pump which was manually operated (much like a grease gun). Guy Raines, who ran the fire department shop, called the company that manufactured it and they sent him the specifications, containing the necessary operating pressures for the equipment to function properly. Raines then devised an electric motor that was connected to a portable generator and when hooked up to the jaws-of-life provided the correct operating pressures for the tool to function correctly. Chief Levy gave the plans for the electric motor to the company in return for two more jaws-of-life. Information on the Tallahassee Fire Department's input for the jaws-of-life was provided by firefighter Mike Knowles and verified by Assistant Chief Ridgway Coe (Retired). The jaws-of-life tool, made by Hurst in 1972, was a two-part system consisting of a 32-inch hydraulic spreader powered by a two cycle gasoline power unit. When activated, the scissor-like spreaders opened and forced crushed metal away from trapped victims. Because the tool reduced the time to extricate a victim from a car crash, literally snatching them from the "jaws of death," the tool earned the name Jaws of Life. Actually, Horrie Culpepper Jr., whose CB handle was "Rescue 1" was the first person to have this particular piece of equipment in Tallahassee. Culpepper was a civilian who loved to help others. He responded to both police and fire calls and would do whatever was asked of him. His vehicle was the best-equipped emergency response vehicle in the county.

b. First fire department to put water on their apparatus. Levy had 150-gallon tanks installed on the pumpers, which gave an instant water source at fire scenes. Often this is all that was needed to extinguish a small fire. Other fire departments laughed at this but now it is common practice to have 500 or 1000 gallon water tanks on fire engines. It should be noted that Chief Coe had a small water tank installed in his Chief's car for the same reasons.

c. Pre-connected hoses. Generally, hose lengths were rolled up in 50' sections. They had to be unrolled and then connected using couplings. The use of pre-connected hose saved quite a bit of time and man power when taking the hose off the truck at a fire. The hose was systematically laid in the hose bed to permit the sections to be coupled together in such a fashion to allow off-loading of the hose without the hose getting tangled up.

d. First double-cab fire engine. Chief Levy was very shrewd when he hired new personnel. He would not only look for men who could do the firefighting job but also for men who had other talents. William "Guy" Raines (Assistant Chief, February 25, 1942- June 1, 1977) had a degree from Georgia Tech in engineering and was an expert in designing and making apparatus parts on the lathe. James Swearingen (Captain, February 1, 1947- January 31, 1983) was known for his skill as a welder and welded the first double-cab fire truck for the department. Tommy "T.E." Roberts (District Chief, June 2, 1950-January 21, 1991) was an excellent painter. Sidney Stoutamire (Assistant Chief, March 30, 1944-March, 31, 1977) was an excellent body man. These individuals and several other firefighters were responsible for making the fire trucks from the chassis up, including the equipment that went on the trucks. They also did all repairs to the apparatus.

e. Chief Levy knew what he wanted on a fire truck and how he wanted it to function. He also was keenly aware of his budget limitations. He could afford to buy a fire truck but not one that was fully equipped. He would purchase parts and then have the fire department shop build the fire truck. When Station 2 was opened at 224 E 6th Avenue, a shop was built into the back of the station on ground level. Five or six fire trucks were built at this location between 1951 and the early 1960s. Newly purchased vehicles were stripped down to the chassis and rebuilt to Levy's specifications. Five of the vehicles were:

Unit 11 and Unit 12 built on a Ford chassis, housed at the main station.

Unit 23 and 24 built on an International chassis, at Fire Station 4.

Unit 6 was housed at Fire Station 4.

Chief Levy was a very educated man, with his best knowledge coming from personal observations and investigations of true life situations.

Anytime or anywhere a community had a tragic situation where the Fire Service was involved, he immediately visited the scene, where he observed the state of affairs and talked with the Incident Commander (fire officer in charge of the scene). Levy never criticized the efforts of those in control; therefore all who knew him would freely discuss their failures as well as any successes in handling situations. He traveled extensively for fire related matters, having visited all states on the mainland, plus Canada and Mexico. Whenever possible he visited fire departments, large and small, where he exchanged information with those he met.

Chief Levy was always taking notes when others were lecturing. He carried a pencil not over two inches long so people would not borrow it. When people did ask to borrow his pencil, they always returned it to him; it was so short and stubby that nobody kept it. However, he seldom had notepaper. He would write on road maps, table napkins, banquet tickets, or any other object present. He accumulated many humorous comments for his files.

Between 1935 and 1977, Levy received 45 certificates and/or diplomas for courses, sessions, training seminars and workshops. He also believed in having his men trained.[9]

Chief Levy not only learned from others but was more than willing to share his knowledge in the furtherance of the fire service. He was a real mentor to former Maryland State Fire Marshal Robbie Robertson, from Robbie's college days at what was then, Oklahoma A & M College. The relationship continued thru his 18 years as State Fire Marshal of Maryland, where he served five governors of both parties. While Chief Robertson was serving in Gainesville,

---

[9] An in-service training syllabus used by Tallahassee Fire Department personnel during Chief Levy's tenure can be found in Appendix E. (pg. 128)

Alachua County, Chief Levy stayed at his house to address the Fellowship of Christian Firefighters Chapter.

On January 25, 1925, Chiefs T. P. Coe of Tallahassee, Tom Haney of Jacksonville, Rutledge Smith of South Jacksonville, C.P. Townsend of St. Augustine, B.B. Hart of Daytona, E.F. Beville of Gainesville, F.C. Pfhaender of Winter Haven, A.P. Sadler of West Palm Beach, and R. N. Hershey of Lake Worth Fire Department met in Jacksonville, Florida and organized the Florida State Firemen Association. They formed the association for the sole purpose of bettering the conditions of the fire service and protection of life and property in the state of Florida. The organization continues to exist today. Newspapers document the organizations existence as far back as 1926 with members throughout the state and over 500 attending its conferences.[10]

Levy was well-known throughout the fire service, and was often requested to serve in prominent chairman and leadership positions. He often declined speaking engagements because of other commitments, but was always willing to serve in the background. He was a member of the International Association of Fire Chiefs and International Fire Service Training Association. He also served as chairman of the Educational Committee of State Fire Chiefs, at a time when the committee was of great help in getting college-level Fire Service education made available and Associate Degrees granted. Delmar Publishers recognized Levy's expertise, and in early 1974 requested that he write a textbook aimed at the two-year college market.[11] In his sister, Jeanette's, words "Earl explored every facet of firefighting and

---

[10] It is interesting to note that in 1940 the annual fee for their monthly publication *Florida Fireman* was 5 cents.

[11] See Appendix D for a copy of the publisher's letter requesting him to write a textbook (pg. 114)

firefighting equipment available throughout the United States, especially the South. He "learned" it, then "taught" it locally, at the State Fire College and Junior Colleges all over the South. He was in great demand as a speaker and teacher."

Levy was a hospitable man. No fire service personnel ever visited the Tallahassee Fire Department without him taking them on a tour of fire apparatus and facilities or having a chief officer do so; and, if possible, he insisted they have a meal together, at his expense. Chief Robbie Robertson remembers spending the night on a cot in Levy's office, having stopped by from his home in Orlando while motoring to Stillwater, Oklahoma, where he was in an academic fire protection program. But the Chief's hospitality was not limited to fire department personnel. Robert W. Carter, the city's first executive director of personnel and training went on an in-service tour with Levy, shortly after Robert was hired, to St. Petersburg and Lakeland, Florida in late July or early August, 1973. Upon their return, Carter wrote a letter to Levy expressing his gratitude. Carter stated, "I especially enjoyed the wholesome, positive attitudes that you have concerning your fellow man, fellow workers and your overall expertise in the area of Fire Fighting, Safety, Management and Personnel relations".[12]

---

[12] See Appendix D, for Mr. Carter's letter (pg. 113)

On April 23, 1961, Tallahassee Regional Airport began operations as Tallahassee Municipal Airport. The first Station 5 was built in 1961 and closed on Nov 2, 1998. Nov. 24, 1961. Photo Courtesy of; State Archives of Florida, Florida Photographic Collection

Levy was proactive in fire prevention. He knew that fires are caused in various ways and would try and increase the public's knowledge of fires in an effort to reduce the number of fires caused by heating appliances. On December 8, 1945, in an article that appeared in the *Tallahassee Democrat*, Chief Levy warned the public about the use of heaters and gave several safety precautions against heaters and chimney fires. He closed by stressing that every family needs to have an exit plan.[13] Levy also had articles published in the *Panarama of Progress*. *Panarama of Progress* was published monthly by the City of Tallahassee for city residents, citizens and employees to read. The April 1966 issue contained several articles on the fire department and fire safety including: "Fire Dept. has Good Year in '65," "Training and Fire Prevention Pays," "Tallahassee's Fire Rating Good," "Levy Submits Annual Report," and "Chief Levy Serves Capital City 39 years."[14]

---

[13] See Appendix E for the complete *Tallahassee Democrat* article (pg. 130)
[14] See Appendix E, for April 1966 issue of *Panarama of Progress* (pg. 131)

Jeanette stated, "He truly exhibited the trait of "locking in" with the Tallahassee Fire Department, exploring every facet of firefighting and equipment available throughout the United States, especially the South. He "learned" it, then "taught" it locally, at the State Fire College and Junior Colleges all over the south. He was in great demand as a speaker and teacher. We all were so very proud of him! His 38 years as Tallahassee Fire Chief demanded his all, and he sincerely gave it."

Chief Levy on Deck Gun
Photo Courtesy of; State Archives of Florida, Florida Photographic Collection

"I remember, so well, his top priority in the early days was having equipment and expertise to fight and win-over fires at Elberta Crate Factory and at FSU and Florida A&M Universities. The minute the two-story buildings began to be planned/erected on the college campuses, he was focused on it." (J. Fountain)

A unique method used to present fire prevention during Chief Levy's tenure. This picture was most likely taken during Fire Prevention Week, which is the first full week in October of each year since 1951. *Foreground,* Chief Wynn (on bumper); *background, left to right:* unidentified firemen, Bernard Guedry, Clyde Lee, unidentified fireman.
Photo courtesy of Carol Albertson, Deputy Chief Ed Wynn's daughter.

"Chief Levy stayed "hip-to-hip" with Arvah Hopkins, Tallahassee's city manager whenever building plans were reviewed. He studied all plans for new buildings and those which would expand the City of Tallahassee.

He threw his support into being ready for the airport and its changing uses; and made sure "his men" were capable and best prepared for fighting this new type of fire (aircraft fires). His firefighters knew and felt his knowledge and support for them." (J. Fountain)

When Chief Levy received the "Good Government" award in 1955, he was praised for his "countless" speeches before various groups on behalf of fire prevention and safety. [15]

The main fire station, Station 1, was located at 109 S. Adams Street. The Fire Department moved into this two-story structure in 1937 and closed July 4, 1971. According to Deputy Chief Herb Roberts, "There was no central air and heat so it was hot as hell in the summer and cold as the North Pole in the winter." Photo Courtesy of, State Archives of Florida, Florida Photographic Collection

---

[15] See Appendix E, for complete newspaper article (pg.133)

Chief Levy, *left,* with his life-long friend and Tallahassee Volunteer Fire Company member May Walker (TVFC, 1923-1926) who left the volunteers to go to law school, and eventually became Judge Walker.
Photo courtesy of Assistant Chief Ridgway Coe (Retired)

9

Rediscovered History

Chief Levy retired in January 1978, but made one last contribution to the Tallahassee Fire Department. Information about a significant piece of fire history was amongst his papers. The history of Tallahassee's fire bell and the bell itself would have been lost had Levy not written a letter to Mrs. Joe Kittrell at Immanuel Baptist Church, providing her with information on its past. [16]

In 1896, a bell three feet in diameter, 32" high and weighing 1500 pounds was installed in the tower of the Market Place building when it was built on the southeast corner of Adams and Jefferson streets. When the fire alarm box was pulled, it sent a signal to the fire station indicating the fire district in which the fire alarm box was located. The gear box was manually set to the fire district number where the fire alarm box was located. The gear box was placed in the bell controller and electrical impulses were sent to a rigid hammer that rang the bell. For instance, if a fire alarm box in fire district 14 was pulled, the bell would ring one long ring and 4 short ones. This would be repeated automatically 4 or 5 times, with proper intervals in-between rings. Likewise, if a telephone call was received, the fire district was determined from the address given, the gears set and the bell rung. All the firemen, and everyone else in the city, would know which district the fire was in and respond to that area. When the Market Place was demolished, the bell was placed in storage. On February 9, 1947, City Fire Inspector and former Fire Chief T.P. Coe was present when the bell was installed in the tower of Immanuel Baptist Church located, where the Civic Center stands as of the early 21st century. Immanuel Baptist Church rang the bell for services for many years, and then relocated it to the spire of their church at 2351 Mahan Drive, when it was built on February 17, 1976.

---

[16] See Appendix E for Chief Levy's letter to Mrs. Kittrell. (pg. 135)

10

"The Chief" and "His Men"

It was apparent that the City of Tallahassee Fire Department was his family, when Levy spoke of his firemen with paternal pride in his high pitched voice. Chief Levy loved and appreciated his firemen friends, as can be seen in his letters to those who were retiring from the department, his comments on their service and the ISO rating.

When Assistant Chief Clyde Johnson retired in 1956, Levy noted in a letter, that Clyde's retiring not only left a deep gap in the fire department but also as a personal friend. [17]

Morris Wainwright served as a hands-on and invaluable assistant chief during the months when Chief Levy was confined to bed with rheumatic fever. He was appointed the department's first deputy chief on February 1, 1957, and served in that capacity until his retirement in 1966. At that time, Levy named him an Honorary Lifetime Deputy Chief and presented him with the badge that he had worn with loyalty and competence, feeling that no one else should ever wear it.[18]

At the City Commission meeting in December 1977, Chief Levy presented retiring Deputy Chief James Cureton the Distinguished Service Award. Levy gave an emotional speech praising Cureton as a fearless man who had often

---

[17] See Appendix D for complete letter (pg. 117)
[18] See Appendix D, for complete letter (pg. 118)

risked his life fighting fires, saying, "There has never been a more dedicated, loyal, and valuable person to the citizens of Tallahassee." [19]

Crediting former firemen, Chief Levy said "No man is sufficient unto himself. There have been many people who gave their lives to create the kind of department we have now. I meet the living members of the old volunteer fire department on the street, and they are proud of the kind of fire department we have today."[20]

Chief Levy ordered a new air conditioned Chevrolet Suburban for Deputy Chief Ed Wynn, but Chief Wynn became seriously ill and was hospitalized before it arrived. On a Sunday afternoon, one day before Wynn's scheduled operation, Levy picked Wynn up at the hospital and took him home to see his family. Chief Wynn got to ride in his new air conditioned vehicle, but never drove it. He did not regain consciousness after the operation, and died soon thereafter. He rests in Tallahassee's Roselawn Cemetery.

Fred Mitchell served 29 years on the Tallahassee Fire Department (August 16, 1946-August 15, 1975). At a ceremony on Mitchell's last day with the fire department, Chief Levy appointed him an Assistant Chief and presented him with a retirement plaque reading the same.[21]

Chief Levy not only loved and respected his employees, he respected and defended firemen everywhere. He served as Director for the Florida State Firemen's Association for many years, actively participated in group training in the early days, and assisted in drafting and passage of Chapter 175, the Florida State Firemen's Pension and Retirement Act. He took particular interest and

---

[19] See Appendix D for complete letter regarding Deputy Chief James Cureton (pg. 119)
[20] Tallahassee Gazette, April 10, 1974
[21] See Appendix D for entire letter (pg. 120)

pride in the Florida State Fire College and its contribution to fire service training statewide, and served as one of the first three trustees for that institution.

Chief Levy thought that firefighting equipment had gotten progressively better throughout the years, but that conditions firemen faced when fighting fire were in some respects worse. In the 1974 *Tallahassee Gazette* article, he commented "These modern buildings are filled to overflowing with electrical appliances; the fire potential is staggering." He credited sprinkler systems as one of the best of all fire prevention devices. "The alarm goes off and the sprinkler immediately goes to work and drowns the fire before it has a chance to spread," Levy continued. "If I had to name one modern fire prevention device that would have to be it." He was probably referring to a "deluge" fire sprinkler system consisting of pipes running just below ceiling level throughout a building with open sprinkler heads attached to it. The piping was connected to a water supply. When activated by heat detectors, the valve keeping the water from flowing through the pipe opened, and allowed water to simultaneously discharge through all the sprinkler heads onto the fire.

Chief Levy was also fond of telling the firemen that they were like spokes on a wheel. If you remove a spoke, the wheel will still turn but it cannot turn without the wheel's hub. He also let them know that he was the hub of the wheel.

Levy was a Christian man, but he was also unmistakably the Chief of the Tallahassee Fire Department, and he alone was authorized to interact with the city commissioners, mayor, press and the public. One day in the early 1950s, during the time employees could be fired without cause, a city commissioner called the main station and asked to speak with a relatively new firefighter who had a side business trimming trees. Levy answered the phone in his office and then stayed on the line while the man took the call in the day room. The details of the conversation between the fireman and commissioner are not known, but when the fireman later went to report on the nature of the call, Levy looked him in the eye and said that he already knew. The fireman subsequently transferred to the Tallahassee Police Department. He retired from that organization as a captain.

Chief Levy once walked out into the truck bay and asked a fireman how many "Fire Chiefs" the department had. Since there were three assistant chiefs and one deputy chief, as well as Chief Levy, the fireman answered that there were five. Levy said "No, there is only one Fire Chief and that is me." Even today, anyone who has been around the fire department for any length of time knows this to be true without having to verbalize it. This was demonstrated when a reporter came to the fire department and asked Chief Levy if he could talk to the men. The two went to the day room where all the firefighters were gathered together. The reporter would ask a question and Levy would provide the answer. This went on and on until finally, the reporter asked him if was ever going to let anyone else answer a question. Levy politely said that since all the questions that he had asked so far involved decisions that were ultimately his to make as Fire Chief, he had answered them without having to first go through someone else.

Chief Levy was demanding, but also cared very much for his employees as evidenced in his meeting notes for an "All Personnel" meeting he held on September 14, 1966. Deputy Chief Morris Wainwright, the first Tallahassee deputy chief, had resigned from the fire department due to health issues. Levy promoted Lieutenant Edgar "Ed" Wynn to deputy chief. Promotion from lieutenant to deputy chief is not the usual progression, Wynn had been in charge of the training center and recommended that the old Dale Mabry airfield control tower be relocated to behind fire Station 4, which saved the department the cost of buying a new training tower.

During the meeting of "All Personnel", Chief Levy stressed the point that he promoted the most qualified person to deputy chief and that he would not tolerate any insubordination towards either Deputy Chief Morris Wainwright, while he was still here, or to Lieutenant Ed Wynn. He ordered Lieutenant Wynn to inform him of any insubordination or "school boy" tricks, and promised to deal with such harshly. At this meeting Levy also announced new criteria for promotions, where "education" would be a primary consideration. [22]

Chief Levy sent his retirement request to City Manager Daniel A. Kleman on November 30, 1977. In it he praised past and present fire department personnel and stated that the Department has reached a very high level of efficiency and development that can only be maintained through the cooperation of the community. On March 9, 1979, Levy sent a letter to his good friend Fire Marshal James C. Robertson, state of Maryland, regarding his retirement. Levy stated "No man could ever have a more rewarding career than I had, and it was wonderful to know that even with my 67 years of age our young 31-year-old city manager shed tears when I left. Also, he did as I asked him to and appointed the man I wanted as Chief."[23]

Mrs. Melba Jones, Chief Levy's secretary for 28 years, had the following to say in the *1974 Tallahassee Gazette* article regarding Levy leaving the Fire Department: "Someday he is going to walk out of this office for good and when that man retires his shoes are going to be mighty hard to fill."

---

[22] It is interesting to note that the emphasis on education continues into the 21st century. Under Fire Chief Cindy Dick, Fire Officer 1 certification through the State Fire College is now required to be promoted to Lieutenant.

[23] See Appendix D for both letters (Kleman pg. 121) (Robertson pg. 123)

11

Accomplishments

Chief Levy's accomplishments include:

1940 – After succeeding Fire Chief T. P. Coe, Levy became a member of the Florida State Firemen's Association. Throughout the years, he served on the Board of Directors, and remained a member of this organization until he retired.

1946 – 1950 (probably in this time-frame). He was one of the early-day graduates in college-level Municipal Fire Administration, which was offered by the Institute for Training in Municipal Administration. They also published books on Civil Defense Training such as *Civilian Defense: Suggestion for State and Local Fire-Defense* (1941 - 27 pages). Reese Revell Jr., Assistant Chief (August 1, 1952- January 6, 1985) in a letter to

Left to Right: Assistant Chiefs; Clyde Johnson, Morris Wainwright, Chief Levy in Center, George McDaniel, J.B. Harvey, 1951. Photo Courtesy of; State Archives of Florida, Florida Photographic Collection

Chief Levy on why he wanted to be a fireman cited the course on civil defense and its teaching of fire department work for his keen interest in becoming a fireman. Reese had thought that all firemen just sat around and did nothing but found out differently in the Civil Defense Class.

1949 – Legislature created a law by which the Florida Fire College became a permanent state institution. On September 15, 1949, Chief Levy was appointed by Secretary of State, R. A. Gray to serve with Bill Barnett and Tom Sexton on the first Board of Trustees of the Florida State Fire College. Although Levy was reluctant to serve because he knew it would require a great deal of his time and effort, he accepted the position because he recognized the impact that institution could have on the fire service. The Board was appointed and developed plans for construction and implementation of various aspects of the law authorizing the establishment of the Florida State Fire College. He was reappointed on October 23, 1950, then again on January 8, 1951, serving until October 4, 1953. Upon each reappointment, Governor Fuller Warren sent Levy a personal letter wishing him a most successful term of office. However on May 13, 1952, Levy sent a letter to the governor resigning from the Board, due to personal reasons.

1954 – Chief Levy taught classes on "Fire Department Administration" at the Florida Fire College in June and August of 1954. Mr. W. H. Barnett, superintendent of the Florida State Fire College wrote the following to Levy after the Chief taught the class in June: "We can never tell you how much we appreciate what you have done for us in helping us out in this pinch. Although I was not here, I understand from several sources that you did a grand job."

1954 – Chief Levy served as chairman of the Committee on Fire Department Administration for the Florida Fire Service Training Improvement Conference, sponsored by the Florida State Fire College.

1955 – W. Fred Heisler was a consultant to Oklahoma A&M College (later Oklahoma State University). His work on firefighting had been adopted by 26 states and four Canadian provinces. He and Chief Levy attended a two-day Conference of Southeastern Fire Officials, discussing material for a textbook on preplanning firefighting tactics for various types of structures. Levy also reviewed and provided input on other fire-related subjects and proposed subject matter. He was an instrumental member of "Special Committees," whose input was used in fire service training manuals later prepared at Oklahoma A&M College for the International Fire Service Training Association. These manuals were often referred to as "Red" books because the covers were red in color. (March 17, 1955, *Greensboro Record*)

1955 – Received the "Good Government Award" from the Junior Chamber of Commerce in Tallahassee, Florida. This was an annual award given to a government official whose diligence goes beyond his ordinary responsibility. In presenting the certificate, Rufus Jefferson, chairman of the award recipient committee, cited Chief Levy's "courage and outstanding accomplishment in the field of good government."

1957 – He was a member of the two-man committee that wrote the by-laws establishing the present Florida Association of Fire Chiefs. Chief Charlie M. Deal of Lakeland was its first president in 1958-1959, and Chief Levy served as president in 1967-1968.

1957 – He received the Cooper-Taylor Memorial Award, given by the Florida Junior Chamber of Commerce for promoting public safety. The nature of questions posed to Chief Levy, and his answers, provide additional insight about him.

1. Question: What do you consider important in life and most worth working towards?

    Answer: My firm belief in God is the most important thing to me. Within this personal conviction lies the belief that every Christian should develop his life to its fullest potential. My life's work has centered around fire protection. My motivation was in this direction, personally and through other people.

2. Question: Who gave you the original inspiration for your current activities and interests?

    Answer: My greatest inspiration came from W. Fred Heisler, an early-day Training Specialist and teacher from Oklahoma State University. He was a great <u>personal</u> <u>friend</u> and instructor. Also, a Dale Carnegie course under Carnegie personally, I feel had a great bearing.

3. Question: What do you consider the most important ingredient in your professional career?

    Answer: The ability to appreciate the efforts of others and adaptability to changes when necessary or advantageous.

4. Question: What future do you see for safety promotion in Florida?

    Answer: It is obvious that renewed emphasis is being put on all phases of public safety, and undoubtedly, this trend <u>will</u> <u>continue</u> and be <u>intensified</u>.

1957 – He received the Woodmen of the World Award for Community Service. Woodmen of the World is a life insurance organization founded in Omaha, Nebraska on June 6, 1880. In 1953 it established an award to recognize conservationists and environmentalists.

1957 – Fire Department Instructors Conference. The first international-level Fire Department Instructors Conference was held in 1928 in Chicago and eight people attended. In fifty-seven, Chief Levy attended and appeared on the program of that year's four-day annual conference, held in Memphis, Tennessee, a forum where 2,009 leaders in modern firemanship and training gathered to keep abreast of the latest developments. Each presentation was monitored by a traffic light on stage that flashed green when the speakers' time started, then amber with one minute remaining and turned red when the speakers' allotted time was up. This ensured that each instructor received his full allotted time to properly present his topic.

The subject was "How to Better Protect the Lives and Property of the Nation from Fire." [24] Chief Levy sat on the Fire Instructors Panel at this conference. They could not have had a better expert on fire prevention to sit on the panel along with four other fire chiefs.

1962-1963 – Served as president of the 10-state Southeastern Association of Fire Chiefs, which was part of the International Association of Fire Chiefs. Chief Levy was the first vice president of the association and was the unanimous choice for president of the Association by the delegates to the 34th Annual Conference.

1964 - Received a Distinguished Service Award from State Fire Marshal, J. Edwin Larson.

1966 – Cited by State Treasurer and Insurance Commissioner Broward Williams, for his assistance to the State. In a letter to Chief Levy, Commissioner Williams stated, "Our mutual cooperation will be the greatest single factor in solving the future problems of our state. You have helped us to move ahead in our many programs and will be extremely beneficial to us in assuring their continued success."

1967-1968 – President, Florida State Fire Chiefs Association. He remained a member of the organization throughout his career and also served as Chaplain of the Association for a number of years.

1969 – Under a contract with the International Association of Fire Chiefs, the Florida State Board of Forestry sponsored meetings with the U. S. Forest Service and all fire service organizations in Florida to develop

---

[24] See Appendix E for more on Levy's presentation (pg. 134)

a prototype model Rural-Urban Fire Defense Plan for the state. The plan was made available to the Federal Office of Civil Defense for use as a guide elsewhere in the nation. Representing the Florida Fire Chief's Association, Chief Levy served along with fifteen others on a review committee that assisted in developing the plan.[25]

1970 – "Earl Levy Day" proclaimed in Tallahassee.

Tallahassee Mayor-Commissioner Lee A. Everhart proclaimed Tuesday, May 5, 1970, "Earl Levy Day." Business leaders of the community sponsored an appreciation banquet, which was attended by more than 300 community leaders.[26]

1970 – The Leon Board of County Commissioners passed a resolution recognizing Chief Levy for his 30 years of dedicated, efficient and effective service to county citizens.[27]

1970 – On May 5th the Tallahassee Insurance Association of Independent Agents staged an appreciation dinner for Chief Levy. He received a plaque marking his 30th anniversary as chief with the Tallahassee Fire Department which cited his dedication to conservation of life and property. The Tallahassee Chamber of Commerce also presented him with a Certificate of Appreciation. Among the special guests were: Ralph Proctor, Theo Proctor, Jack Yeager Sr., Sam Wahnish, Henry Palmer, George E. Lewis Sr., Burr Ragsdale and Hantz Barineau – all former volunteer firefighters who served with Levy. It was typical of Levy to give credit to others. Speaking about the firefighters on May 8th, Levy stated, "I believe in them and they believe in me."

---

[25] It is interesting to note that the monthly bulletin published in 1969 by the U.S. Civil Defense Council was available at an annual subscription rate of $4. 30 per copy or 20 cents for 10 or more mailed in bulk to one address.
[26] See Appendix C for complete proclamation (pg. 102)

[27] See Appendix C, for complete Resolution (pg. 103)

Deputy State Fire Marshal William Thomas Knight said, "He has received practically every honor a fire chief could receive at local, state, national and international levels. As a citizen, I thank him for making Tallahassee a better and safer place in which to live."

State Representative John J. Savage of Pinellas County has known Chief Levy for 17 years and said, "With all the unrest in the nation, it is fine to be associated with a man of his stability, courage and day-in, day-out dedication."

The Westcott Building on FSU's campus caught fire Monday, April 28, 1969. This displaced both FSU offices and students residing in the building. This picture shows students sleeping in front of Bryan Hall on May 23, 1969. Bryan Hall was also used for emergency offices following the Westcott fire. Photo Courtesy of; State Archives of Florida, Florida Photographic Collection

1970 – By unanimous vote, the Florida Senate passed Senator Mallory Horne's Resolution citing Chief Levy for meritorious and outstanding service to the State of Florida and his community. [28]

1971 – Chief Levy was cited by Department of Agriculture Commissioner Doyle Conner for the excellent fire protection provided to all state buildings in Tallahassee and Leon County.

1973-74 – Chief Levy was listed in "Who's Who in the South and South West," 13th Edition.

1974 – Chief Levy received a plaque from Independent Insurance Agents for his "diligence, foresight, planning and hard work." The accompanying resolution read, "Chief Earl Levy has dedicated his entire life to his profession and has gained the respect of fire chiefs nationwide and the reputation as a leader in his field".

1974 – Chief Levy was a member of the committee that put on a dinner for Tallahassee's City Manager, Arvah B. Hopkins. Mr. Hopkins sent a letter to Chief Levy regarding his appreciation for the banquet: "There is no way to express in words appropriate thanks to you or the other members of the committee who put on the dinner for me. I accept this great honor with gratitude and humility. As you well know, no man has any greater possession than his friends. This banquet was something that I will treasure more than anything that has ever happened to me. Thank you again for such a memorable occasion."

1975 – Chief Levy was the first municipal employee named Public Administrator of the Year by the Florida Chapter of the American Society for Public Administration. In making the presentation, long-

---

[28] See Appendix C for Senate Resolution 1373 (pg. 105)

time state worker and retired Director of the Florida Department of Administration, Ken Ireland, recognized the chief as instrumental in Tallahassee's Class 2 insurance rating, and in originating the city's training program, a "model for all fire departments."

Mr. Ralph E. Proctor, Sr. and Chief Levy served together on the city's Volunteer Fire Company, and they have been friends for many years. Mr. Proctor expressed his personal pleasure that Chief Levy had been named Public Administrator of the Year, and offered his congratulations. See Appendix D for Mr. Proctors'[29] letter and Chief Levy's response[30].

1976 – Named the Outstanding Fire Chief in Florida for 1976 by the State of Florida Fire Chief's Association.

1976 – Chief Levy received the Cooper-Taylor Award for outstanding public service.

1976 – Florida Senate Commends Chief Levy and the Tallahassee Fire Department

Senate President Dempsey Barron's aide had to trick Chief Levy to get him anywhere near the capitol complex. He requested that Chief Levy confer with the Senate on some building inspection regulations. Chief Levy said that he worked only for the City of Tallahassee, kept his nose out of state government, and as a matter of policy never spoke to House or Senate committees. The aide assured him that it would just be a little private chat.

On that basis Chief Levy agreed to the meeting, but soon found himself seated at the rostrum as the full Senate passed Resolution 1373[31] sponsored by Pat Thomas and Dempsey Barron. Chief Levy and the Fire Department were commended for efficiency in fire prevention and control, a major factor in the city's outstanding fire insurance rating of

---

[29] Letter from Mr. Proctor (pg.115)

[30] Letter of response from Chief Levy (pg. 116)

[31] Senate Resolution 1373 (pg. 106)

class 2. A rating of class 1 has never been awarded; a rating of 2 has been achieved by only 38 other cities nationwide, and none in Florida.

Also cited was the manner in which firefighters expertly evacuated elderly residents from the 12-story Georgia Bell Dickson Apartments, extinguished the fire without loss of life or serious injury, and "afterward humbly knelt to thank God for His assistance."

1977 – At the request of Congressman Don Fuqua, a Tallahassee Democrat Editorial to commend and congratulate Chief Levy on his 50th anniversary with the Fire Department was printed in section E1833 of the U.S. Congressional Record.[32] Chief Levy was cited for his dedication and the work he had done in furtherance of the Fire Service. Congressman Fuqua sent Chief Levy a personal letter of tribute,[33] referencing his unequaled record of accomplishments

1977 – He was selected for the first "Fire Chief of the Year" award from the Florida State Fire Chiefs Association.

1978 – Distinguished Service Award from Kiwanis Club. He was a member for more than 25 years.

1978 – Citizen of the Year Award from the Elks Club. He also attained Life Membership Status.

---

[32] Congressional Record E1833 (pg107)

[33] Congressman Don Fuqua's letter (pg. 109)

B-25 Airplane Crash at Dale Mabry Air Field. Chief Levy *(white shirt, forefront)*. There were two fatalities as a result of the crash. Photo Courtesy of; State Archives of Florida, Florida Photographic Collection.

On September 28, 1978, Fire Station 1 at 327 N. Adams Street was named the William Earl Levy, Sr. Headquarters Building. At the same ceremony, Chief Levy was made an official lifetime Fire Chief of the City of Tallahassee.[34]

At the Florida Fire Chiefs Association's 29th Annual Conference, July 20-23, 1986, held in Dade County, Florida, the Association paused to remember the brother chiefs who had passed from this life during the past year, with a resolution. They recognized those members for their untiring efforts on the Association's behalf and on that of their communities by helping to preserve life and property. Chief Levy was among those honored.[35]

---

[34] See Appendix D for the proclamation (pg. 125)

[35] See Appendix C for Resolution (pg. 110)

"Earl was energetic in his love of his lord, family, the Fire Department, music, Tallahassee (every aspect), horseback riding, hunting, fishing, and his many, many friends. His daily objective was to be honest and true." (J. Fountain)

Earl Levy was a citizen. He was loyal to Tallahassee, Leon County, and the State of Florida. Viewing for Chief Levy was at Culley & Sons Guardian Funeral Home Chapel. Contributions were requested to go to the "Together We Build Fund," First Baptist Church, where he was a member. He was buried on Friday, April 25, 1986, in the family plot at Oakland Cemetery. He rests there now with his loving wife Hassell next to him.

"Mom used to say that Dad was her #1 boy, I was her #2 boy, and Rick was her #3 boy… she used those (numbers) for her speed dial, but after Dad died, only the #2 and #3 listings were displayed. There would never be another #1 for her, or for the rest of our family." (B. Levy)

The Tallahassee Fire Department would probably agree.

Yes, Chief Levy's noteworthy contributions and his dedication earned him the title, "Dean of the Fire Service."

END

Appendix A

Remembrances

At the request of the author, the Levy family provided input for possible inclusion in this manuscript. This input was essential in finding out and documenting the family history of Chief Earl Levy. Although not all the provided information was used, it is included here in its entirety. Rick and Jeanette Fountain had already compiled information and kindly shared it with the author. Bill Levy compiled his input and that of Mr. Larry Surles for possible inclusion in the manuscript.

- William "Bill" Levy
- Melba Jones – Letter to Bill Levy Regarding Hassell Levy
- Larry Surles – Neighbor
- Rick Levy – Happy Birthday Dad
- Rick Levy – Happy Birthday & Mother's Day
- Jeanette Levy Fountain

William "Bill" Levy Remembrances

My dad, Earl Levy, grew up defending and protecting a family member who had health problems, and he also helped members of my mother's family. Throughout his life he continued to help those who needed assistance; friends, relatives, employees and even strangers.

Daddy liked to hunt quail, and kept his liver and white pointer in a kennel behind the house. One day he came home and found the dog waiting for him in the driveway. Dad looked for a hole in the high kennel fence, but could see nothing amiss. The same thing happened again when Dad happened to be at home. He watched as the dog pressed his back against a small tree just inside the enclosure, used all four feet to climb the fence, and scrambled over the top. Dad soon cut down the tree, and the escape artist was grounded.

Dad also had chickens in a coop behind our house. I became quite attached to them, and helped Mom feed them and gather up fresh eggs, all the while keeping an eye on the aggressive rooster. Things went well until the hens developed a calcium deficiency, and started eating their own eggs to overcome it. They ate quite a few eggs before we could gather them up. Dad mixed ground up oyster shells with the feed as a calcium supplement for the hens, and we were soon able to collect the eggs as before.

One morning Dad and I discovered a hen lying motionless on the ground. He explained that she had been killed by a predator, and dug a hole to bury her. I looked back and forth between dad and the hen – half expecting her to move. She did not, and at that age I didn't understand that she was not going to. As Dad prepared to cover the hen with dirt I said, "Don't hurt her!" He said that she could feel nothing, and explained about the cycle of life. I was sad that she was not going to come back, but finally decided that I could at least remember the time we had spent together; a lesson that I have had to revisit many times through the following years, including when he and Mom died.

Like the rest of the fire department vehicles, Dad's red Chief's car had a two way radio and a siren. He parked it in from of our house when he was home, and one day at about age four, I got the bright idea of very quietly trying the siren out myself. I gently bumped the foot switch, and was pleased that the resulting low moan was not too loud. But the sound persisted for so long that I was afraid dad would hear it. Pushing on the siren brake button would have stopped it from spinning, but I was a bit too scared to experiment further, and decided to see what could be done from outside the car. Fortunately, nobody heard the whirling siren but me, and it had slowed down enough that I wasn't seriously hurt when I stuck my finger in it.

Dad also had a radio monitor at home. When an alarm came in at night he listened for the location and nature of the fire, and evaluated the potential for property damage and danger to his men. Depending on what he learned from radio traffic or concluded on his own, he would either contact the station for more information, dress immediately and go to the scene of the fire, or go back to bed.

Dad's personal car was parked in the driveway when not in use, and was also equipped with a two-way radio. I had often been with him when he was paged and took the microphone from its holder on the dash and responded.

One day I got in the car by myself and turned on the radio to monitor the traffic. Things must have been a bit slow, since it was not long before I picked up the microphone. I was pretty proud of myself for remembering his call sign and said, "Calling Car 14. Calling Car 14, come in," which was what I heard when we were in his city car and someone was trying to reach him; I vaguely wondered why he did not respond.

I was happy to see him drive up soon thereafter, and was so young and naïve that I wondered why he didn't seem happy to see me too. When he asked why I had been on the fire department radio, I didn't even understand how he knew about it. I don't remember getting a whipping; I remember the crime, but not the punishment. But I am sure I got a good talking to, and I got the message.

My first fishing trip with Dad was at age four, and I caught four fish! We bought some earthworms and "split shot" lead sinkers at a bait and tackle store. The sinkers came in a flat blue metal container, and Dad pointed out that "Take a Boy Fishing Today" was printed on the back. I thought that the store owner had made them just for us; it took me awhile to realize that he didn't even know we were going fishing that day.

At that time we had no boat, and fished with cane poles from the bank of a small pond in the Apalachicola National Forest. Dad showed me how far up the line to locate the float and sinkers, and how to bait the hook with earthworms. He said that after I got a nibble, I should wait for him to tell me when to set the hook - but he didn't give me any further advice about how hard I should pull in order to set it.

I got my first nibble, and when dad finally said, "Pull him, Son!" I snatched the fish out of the water, over our heads, and onto the bank behind us where it lay flopping around until Dad picked it up. I caught three more fish that day, but I learned from my first mistake, and none of the rest went over our heads. He was proud of me, so I was proud of myself. In the following years I baited my own hooks, we caught more than a few fish together, and I cleaned my share of them.

We had a fireplace in our living room, and I recall many a cold morning when Dad built a roaring fire before I had even gotten out of bed. If he went outside for more firewood, I would often hear the ring of the ax as he cut the wood to size. He finally installed a gas log in the fireplace, but kept the owl-shaped andirons. The owls will always remind me of warm wood fires on cold mornings, and coals that flickered as our family relaxed in the living room after supper. Now many years later, they reside in my oldest daughter's house, but they still bring back memories from my childhood.

Dad spent time with me when he was home from work, and my earliest toys were those that he and I made together. I especially enjoyed learning how to make the types of toys that he played with when he was a boy.

We made a tractor using a pencil-shaped stick, and one of the large wooden spools that had once held Mom's sewing thread. Power came from a rubber band threaded through the hole in the spool, and secured on the other side. Dad showed me how to cut notches in each rim of the spool so that the "wheel" would get better traction. We wound the rubber band up tight, and if all went according to plan, the tractor would move forward when placed on the ground or rug.

Dad mentioned having a popgun when he was my age, and I didn't even know what he was talking about. So he selected several branches from one of the Chinaberry trees across the street from our house, taught me how to make a popgun, and how to use it.

Together Dad and I made a kite like the ones he flew when he was a young boy, and Mom gave us some scraps of material to use for a tail. We first flew the kite in the field across the street from our house; if the tail was too short, the kite would dart from side to side, if it was too long, the kite could not climb much higher than our heads. After some trial and error we got the tail length just right, and the kite soon flew high and steady in the strong wind.

Several days later Mom packed a lunch for us, and we all three went to an open pasture to fly my kite. I recall that it took quite a bit of running to get the kite aloft in the gentle breeze, but after several attempts, we finally had it airborne. Dad showed me how to make it climb higher and higher by pulling repeatedly on the string, then paying out more line. Far above, the long tail swaying from side to side kept the kite steady. We all took turns flying the kite, and then had a nice lunch on the side of a small hill before heading for home.

Dad also showed me how to make another toy that he had played with as a young boy; we used a wooden spool and carpenter's twine to make a helicopter. A propeller blade was fashioned either from metal, or carved from wood, with a hole in the center just big enough to slide over a wooden dowel. Two small headless nails were driven into one end of the spool, and these fit into holes in the propeller. A length of carpenters twine was wrapped around the spool, and a dowel was inserted through the hole in the spool's center. The propeller was then fitted horizontally onto the spool, and a strong and steady pull on the twine launched it spinning up the dowel and high into the air.

One day when and I was 7 or 8 years old our whole family was in the kitchen, and I did something that made Dad say, "Son, I'm going to wear you out!" I realized that he was not threatening me - that was a promise. I got up from the table, ran through the living room, out the front door, down the steps, and into the back yard. Bad move - Dad caught me half way up the hill behind the house. The actual punishment phase is now a blank spot in my memory, but I do remember that as we returned to the kitchen, young Rick asked "Did you get him, Daddy?"

Dad used to periodically visit all the fire stations, and I sometimes explored one or more of the trucks while he was inside with the men. One day at the airport station I grasped the steering wheel on one of the trucks on my way down to the running board, and bumped the horn button by mistake. Unfortunately that blew the siren, which brought quite a few firemen running out to see what was going on. I was caught red handed, and they told me that the unwritten rule was that anyone who mistakenly blew the siren had to buy the beer. Making a dumb mistake was bad enough, but no one in my family drank beer, and I didn't know where I was going to get any.

When I was about ten years old, Dad showed me several battle-scarred wooden tops that he had kept since childhood. Notches cut into the sides made them hum while spinning, and he said that most of their nicks and cuts came from a game that he played when he was a boy. He explained that each contestant placed his top inside a ring drawn in the dirt, and took turns trying to spin theirs and knock other tops out of the circle.

In those days when almost all games still had winners and losers, players who knocked tops out of the circle got to keep them. (Today, fewer and fewer games are still structured so that only the victors are rewarded, and success depends on skill and determination. Some think that is progress; some do not).

Dad showed me how to wind the string around the top, and how to throw it so that it would flip over and land point down, and spin properly. Then he put several magazines on the hard wood living room floor, and we took turns trying to spin the tops on one of them. Dad was good at it, and I was finally successful a few times. I still have my dad's old wooden tops, and will pass them on to family members.

At about age 11, I had been riding a vintage conventional bicycle we found at Grandmother's house; it was well-used even before I got it. After I added many a mile, I began to think maybe I was ready to move up to an "English Bike" with gears, but Dad was not sure I could handle such a high performance machine, and talked about having my bike re-conditioned.

A friend and I each asked Santa for a new bicycle, and with all the confidence of youth we made a pact to meet and go for a nice long ride after Christmas. When I mentioned this plan to Dad, he asked that I tell him some more about my friend. I described him as best I could, and concluded by saying that he was nice and I liked him a lot. Dad asked specifically where my friend lived, and we drove by the house and yard. Dad said not a word; he saw the same things that I did, but understood a lot more.

I woke up Christmas morning, scrambled out of bed, and ran hopefully towards the living room. Leaning on the kickstand and ready to go was a beautiful "English bike".

But there is more to the story. In the days prior to Christmas, Dad had my conventional bike painted and re-conditioned with a new chain and tires. On Christmas day he told me that if my friend didn't get a bike for Christmas, I should offer to let him use it whenever he wanted to, and that is the way things developed.

We rode together often, but things came to an end one day when we were riding rapidly across the side yard of the old Sealy school, now the headquarters building for the Tallahassee Police Department. My friend was in front, looking back over his shoulder at me with a big grin on his face. But the grin disappeared in a hurry when he hit one of the many stumps remaining from the pine trees that had been removed. The collision bent the front rim and spokes all the way up to the axle, threw him over the handle bars, and the bike landed on top of him. My friend wasn't hurt, but the riding days of the dynamic duo were over.

Our Uncle Bill Arnold gave Rick and me each a cute puppy, half Beagle and half Fox Terrier. But they must have favored the Beagle side of the family; they looked like Beagles, they barked like Beagles, and they liked to stand out on the front porch and bay at the moon.

I don't recall that the neighbors ever complained about their nightly chorus, but Dad soon got tired of hearing them. He would go into the kitchen, fill a pot with water, open the back door, and throw water on the dogs. They would quiet down for a while, but they associated both the water and the preparation with punishment. Soon they scrambled down the steps and into the night when they heard the back door open, before Dad could throw the water. So, he started leaving the door open, and throwing the water through the closed screen door, but the dogs soon noticed when he turned the water on to fill the pot, and didn't stick around. So, Dad left the back door open, and filled the pot with water before he went to bed. That worked until the dogs learned to run when they heard the squeak of oak flooring as Dad came through the living room, and there was no way to get around that little problem. The dogs resumed barking at the moon whenever they felt like it, and we finally gave the dogs to people who had more room to raise them.

Several years after the two dogs, Rick had a huge Persian cat. Even though he had little use for most cats, Dad accepted the fact that Mittens was one of the family. Dad returned from a fire late one dark night, and passed a large oak tree that stood beside our unlit walk lined with boxwoods. Right after he got on the walk, Dad sensed and heard something come down the tree with bark flying everywhere. It shot through one side of the hedge, crossed right in front of him and wound up on the front lawn. After Dad had calmed down a bit, he realized it was just Mittens, welcoming him back home from the fire.

Dad loved to fish. When I was still a young boy he taught me to silently paddle a boat on area lakes. He later taught me how to row and control a boat in the swift current of the St. Marks River, and my oldest daughter Cyndi now has the oars that we used, displayed on a wall in her house. He showed me how to slingshot a cricket up under a low hanging limb when fishing with a cane pole, how to use a bait casting reel, and how to place a plug or plastic worm just where I wanted to put it.

We also hunted squirrels in the river swamp, including the area just off the Old Plank Road near Newport. Dad told me that when he was a young boy, his whole family often packed a lunch and drove to the nearby sulfur spring pool, for a day of relaxing and swimming in the ice cold water. Mom and I took a lunch and swam there with relatives several times.

Dad took me to another location in the nearby woods, and showed me a smaller sulfur spring that boiled up through an old concrete pipe sunk vertically in the ground. We each drank some of the water, and repeated that ritual thereafter every time we were in the area. I didn't much like the taste of sulfur water, but I figured if it was good enough for Dad, it was good enough for me.

Years later, I took each of our teenage daughters to the same location. Even though those young ladies no doubt found the nasty pipe and sulfur taste even less appealing than I did at their age, we each drank some of the water, and recalled good times that we had spent with my dad.

Dad was very supportive of me, and Rick when we were growing up. He and I were in a rock band together when he was a teenager, and like many other aspiring musicians of the day Rick had hair that reached about halfway down his back. Dad didn't approve of this hairstyle, but Rick was always squeaky clean, and Dad tolerated the hair because of Rick's many other admirable qualities. On one occasion the three of us were eating lunch in a restaurant, and a lady sitting at a nearby table commented on Rick's appearance. In a voice that was entirely too loud for her own good, she said, "Look at that; I just wish you would look at that young man! He can dress up in a nice suit and tie all he wants, but it won't make up for that hair." Dad's face turned red, but he didn't say anything for about ten seconds. Then in a voice that carried to the far corners of the restaurant (and got the attention of many) he said, "You know, Son, I'm thinking about letting my hair grow out long like yours. And then I think I'll wind it around my head, and pile it way up on top like that lady over there," pointing at the loud-mouthed woman and her beehive hairdo. If she had more to say, she thought better of it; we didn't hear anything else out of her.

Dad went out of town from time to time, and Mom sometimes saw this as an opportunity to get around the fact that he didn't like unsanctioned changes in the familiar surroundings of his home.

Several times I obliged her by painting the living and dining rooms in his absence, but I respectfully refused to be involved in removing the kerosene heater in the hall between the bedrooms while he was out of town, and turning the space into a storage closet. I still remember the conversation; I said "Mother, I love you – but I'm not going to do that to Daddy." This frustrated her, and she said, "Haven't you learned that it's easier to beg forgiveness than it is to get permission?"

Dad's family loved to share practical jokes and surprises, and that environment may have led to his good sense of humor. On one fishing trip, his Uncle Charlie was seated in the bow of the boat. Dad hooked the first fish almost under Charlie's nose, let the fish run long enough for Charlie to take due notice, then pulled it alongside the boat and out of the water. Dad put another fish or two in the boat, and Charlie started getting frustrated; he refused to even look at the fish Dad was catching. He finally got so mad that he wouldn't talk, just started saying, "Dad boot it!" each time a fish was put in the boat. If Charlie had turned around, he might have noticed that dad never took the first fish off of the hook, he was catching the same one over and over.

Dad actually landed the biggest bass that I ever hooked. I was home on leave from the Navy and we were fishing in Lake Jackson's Rhoden Cove. A fish took my plastic worm, and went straight towards the bottom with it. I could not turn the fish, and pressure on the line hardly even slowed it down. Dad peered over the side of the boat deep into the murky water, and said, "Son, it looks like he is hung up on a snag; we may lose him." He looked back again and then said, "Great day! What a fish!!" I could not have landed that fish by myself; Dad leaned over the side and reached so far down into the water that his face almost disappeared. When he came back up, the fish came up with him. We stopped at a grocery store on the way home, and the fish weighed 12 ½ lbs. on their scales. One of the firemen was also a taxidermist, and Dad paid him to mount the fish. He did a great job, and that action-packed mount still hangs on my wall today.

After Dad retired from the fire department, he and I continued to fish Lake Jackson together. On one occasion my plastic worm landed in an open spot of water among a raft of lily pads near the old lime sink. I let the bait settle towards the bottom of the lake before slowly reeling it towards the boat. I felt a light bump on the other end of the line, lowered the rod tip and took up all the slack, then reared back and set the hook. I held the rod high and took up about five turns on the reel, but suddenly the tip bent almost to the water, the reel screamed, and I lost the line that I had retrieved. Dad said, "Pull him, son!" so I did; the reel screamed and I lost line again, and we both figured that I had hooked another monster bass. Dad again said, "Pull him, Son." We finally noticed the water swirling in two different places, about 20 feet apart. My plastic worm was hung up on an old fence line, and the fence posts were swaying each time I pulled on the "fish."

Why would I relate memories of such a seemingly embarrassing incident? Because it was the last time that I fished with my dad. And it reminds me of the way things started out over 25 years earlier, when he took me fishing at age four, and encouraged me by saying, "Pull him, son!"

Although his job was very stressful Dad didn't let it get the best of him, and I don't recall him ever being cross or irritable at home or around our family. I especially remember him singing in the car when our family took trips. (Years later as a supervisor, I understood how having outstanding employees could put someone in more of a singing mood).

Mom and Dad were both most comfortable singing informally, but I don't think they gave themselves enough credit. Mom played the piano well, and they both had good voices. When I was quite young, they would each periodically sing portions of popular songs such as "When Irish Eyes Are Smiling"; On The Banks Of Loch Lomand"; "You Take The High Road" etc; They were both happy when they sang (or perhaps they sang because they were happy.

My friend Larry Surles once surprised me by recalling something about Mom that I had also noticed, but never mentioned to anyone. He said that her brown eyes always sparkled like she had a secret, and just couldn't wait to share it with others. Larry knew my parents well, and we were neighbors for years. Therefore, Rick and I asked him to assist in this narrative from that perspective. I am glad that my friend has good memories of my parents; he was one of their favorites.

(Note: In addition to the profound, gentle lessons about life she imparted to her own two sons and her grandchildren, Hassell Levy taught first graders in Sunday School at First Baptist Church for over thirty years, where she did influence the lives of literally hundreds.)

Mom used to sing the song "When Irish Eyes are Smiling", and hers usually were; like Larry, that's the way I will always remember them.

Mom used to say that Dad was her #1 boy, I was her #2 boy, and Rick was her #3 boy. I noticed that she used those and appropriate phone numbers for her speed dial, but after Dad died, only the #2 and #3 listings were displayed. There would never be another #1 for her, or for the rest of our family.

Melba Jones Remembrances

After Hassell Levy's death in 2000, Bill Levy wrote Chief Levy's long term assistant and friend Melba Jones, who wrote back and shared the following thoughts:

"I met your mother in 1955 and immediately liked her. As I became better acquainted with her, I realized what a really special person she was, and admired her more and more as time went on.

And yes, your father would have been proud of her those last years. But, he was always proud of her and his two sons. Your mother was so good to visit me after I became disabled and her visits always made me fell less lonely. We shared joys and sorrows.

I deeply appreciate your letter to me. I know you miss your mother. I will always treasure my memories of her, and be proud that I was one of her many friends.

                Sincerely yours, Melba"

Larry Surles Remembrances

Sometimes we are fortunate enough to encounter individuals who turn out to be exceptional people and whose influence on our lives causes us to carry memories of them in our hearts as long as we are alive. Nouwen[36] wrote that a caring person is one who was silent with us in a time of despair, who stays with us during grief, and who instead of giving advice, solutions or cures is content to share our pain and touch our wounds with a warm and tender hand. Such people were "Chief" Earl Levy and his dear wife, Hassell Levy, both shining examples of caring individuals and the type of person we all would like to be.

I first met the Levy family when I was about 10 years old. My family had just moved into the neighborhood and their older son, Bill, was quick to introduce himself. Bill and I became fast friends and lifelong buddies, but that is another story. That first day, we played and tossed a football until it was dark, and would have spent the entire night doing so if his mom had not whistled for him. Anytime Mrs. Levy wanted Bill home she whistled. I can hear that whistle to this day, more than 50 years later. It was not a sharp and commanding whistle; it was almost as soft as the call of a Bob While quail; more of a suggestion than a summons. But it was a strong suggestion, and got results.

Mr. and Mrs. Levy seemed to enjoy life and wanted to share it with you. Mr. Levy had the confident look of a man who knew his business, had just heard the funniest story, and seemed to be inwardly smiling to himself. Mrs. Levy had eyes that smiled, inviting you to talk and listen. Her cheerful attitude, reinforced by her sparkling eyes, openly displayed her enthusiasm for life. Each of these people was genuinely glad to see you, to ask about your family, or find out what was happening. They both welcomed me into their home like another member of their family, no matter the time of day. For a long time they were almost surrogate parents to me.

At mealtime another plate was made up for me, even if I had just eaten at home. I learned about new foods from Mrs. Levy. She made pear/lettuce/cheese/mayo salad, spiced luncheon meat sandwiches, and carrot cake that I ate with gusto.

---

[36] Henri Nouwen was a 20th century priest and author.

Once, Mrs. Levy made some carrot cake that was especially delicious, and we devoured it. Before we could get up from the table, I started having one of my allergic reactions, itching and swelling up, and Mrs. Levy was frantic. After I recovered, she told me it scared her so badly she was never making carrot cake for me again! I couldn't figure out why I was suddenly allergic to her carrot cake, until she recalled that she didn't have enough sugar for the recipe and had used saccharin. She was upset that she had caused my reaction, but was glad to know it wasn't the carrots.

Mrs. Levy has a special place in my heart for her caring nature, especially with regard to my mom. When Mom was very sick, Mrs. Levy was quickly on the scene. She called or visited almost every day during Mom's last illness, bringing a dish of some kind, and a positive, cheerful outlook to help Mother get through the day. She went out of her way to make sure I was doing alright, and asked what she could do for me; just telling me she was praying for my mom's recovery was enough.- When I missed seeing Mrs. Levy for several days, I learned she had broken a bone when she tripped and fell on the way to check on Mom. It wasn't long before Mrs. Levy was visiting Mom again, despite her own pain. Imagine such a good neighbor as that!

Good neighbor also describes "Chief" Levy. He was also a Christian in the best sense of the word. By example, manner and a calm and humorous attitude, Mr. Levy always served as a model for me. He never spoke ill of anyone, never made an off-color remark or expressed anger inappropriately. Yet, he told the funniest stories and seemed to enjoy life way beyond most people. Young boys sometimes venture into projects or get into mischief when they should not. When Bill and I did so, Mr. Levy was firm in his correction, but even-tempered and calm, no matter the transgression.

"Chief" Levy took the time to make sure young boys were occupied with wholesome endeavors. He helped us construct a basketball goal behind the house. He took us out to target practice with our .22s or to hunt squirrels, while teaching us gun handling safety and responsibility. I would never have been able to learn such things without him. Mr. Levy let us have fun too. He allowed us to be boys, but made sure we understood the boundaries of good behavior. Even after I was a grown man, Mr. Levy would stop me on the street, say "hello", and ask about Mom, and the family. I will always remember his kindness and support when my dad died unexpectedly. The family, especially Mom, was devastated by the suddenness of the event. Mr. Levy, like a good "Chief", was first on the scene; with words of comfort and caring for my Mom, and prayer for my Dad. During that time of grief, I was consoled by Mr. Levy's presence and quiet support. He went beyond expectations, driving 120 miles round trip several times to Madison, Florida to be with the family at the funeral home and to attend services. Mr. Levy also attended my dad's interment. I was almost numb from grief, but Mr. Levy's firm handshake and comforting words helped me get through the day. That's the person he was – always there when you needed him.

Like Nouwen's caring friend, Mr. and Mrs. Levy had warm and tender hands and a reassuring presence in times of trouble. They brought joy and smiles with them when they came and reached out to help others. How can you not but love and fondly remember such caring people?

Rick Levy – Happy Birthday!

November 10, 1980

Happy birthday! Seventy years. A long time. You've lived a lot of life, born a lot of burdens, shared a lot of joy. You've been honored again and again by any number of people and organizations, for any number of important accomplishments. I want, however, to talk about the most important thing to Bill and me, something which is an ongoing commitment you've never lost sight of. You have been a father. No, not just "fathered" us; been a father to us. You have cared about our needs, and have been there to meet them. You've taught us what it means to be a husband, a father, a man.

Together, you and the most wonderful mother in the world have made us feel like the most – loved sons in the world.

You've shown us that our interests and endeavors are important to the two of you, simply because they're important to us. Football games, basketball games, track meets, PTA meetings, band concerts, singing events…How many hours (hundreds of hours)…? We knew you were there, and we tried that much harder because we knew you were watching.

You've taught us how to love our own children.

You've taught us that money is merely an incidental factor, a certain amount of which is necessary for everyday living, but not at all worth pursuing for its own sake or just for what it can buy. We've seen you give it away time after time to others who needed it more than you.

You've taught us that principles and people are more important than worldly success.

You've taught us that the needs of others are more important than personal comfort. When sacrifices for others have been necessary, you've made them. We've seen you open your very home to a long succession of people who were in need, sometimes for years at a time.

You have taught us that a man can (and should) be both rock – hard and strong in principle, yet totally compassionate and gentle.

You've taught us what forgiveness means.

You've taught us tolerance toward others.

You've given us a love and appreciation for beauty and simplicity: a fire in the fireplace on a cold morning, "acrobatics" on the living room rug, a fishing trip, a sunrise, God's world, a record of George Beverly Shea singing "How Great Thou Art."

You have never, never said one thing and done another. You've lived your religion.

You've taught us to try our best, then trust in God and not ourselves. We've seen you live by Faith ever since we can remember.

You've taught us to admit our imperfections, by admitting your own. You've never claimed to have all the answers, or to be living the perfect life.

You've taught us to think of God in terms of perfect love and forgiveness rather than punishment, and to judge other people as much for their motives as for their behavior.

You've taught us to stand up for our beliefs, even when they may be ridiculed, and you've done it with dignity. We've seen you.

You've taught us to deal with opposition or problems with quiet strength. We have never seen you bluster.

You've taught us that positions of responsibility, honor, and power should be used to serve others, not for selfish gain.

You've taught us never to take advantage of someone weaker than ourselves; to be kind to the "little ones", even to fight for them. We've seen you, over and over. You have inspired others to change their lives. There are many, perhaps hundreds, of people walking this earth who are today somehow better men and women for having known you. We are very aware of this.

You've taught us humility.

You've taught us that it's all right to cry, especially over another person's hurts.

You've given us that singular privilege, all of our lives, of being able to mention to practically anyone in our city who our father is, and to invariably hear the phrase "…A fine man…" and to KNOW that it's true.

We would give up our very lives for you if called upon, just as if that were the most natural thing in the world to do, without a second thought. Think about this, and know what kind of father you are to us. If you had never accomplished those other things you've been honored for; if you had never done, and never do, anything else with your life, just being the father you are to us would qualify you as a great man. WHICH YOU ARE.

We love you, Pop. We thank God for you. And we see more than you might think we see.

Happy birthday. May you have seventy more.

Love, Rick

Rick Levy – Happy Birthday & Mother's Day

May 9, 1981

Dear Mom,

Happy birthday!! Happy Mother's Day!! It's really appropriate that these two events should fall so close together, since for the majority of your 70 years you've always been unofficially "mothering" somebody or other, and in a wonderful way!

Edith, through her adolescent years…Harry and Pat…Two complete "dens" of Cub Scouts (remember the killer bees at Mode Stone's house?)…Innumerable PTA homerooms…Football, Track, and Basketball players…A long succession of rock and roll bands: Garry, Paul, Glenn, Freddie, and Don (remember the infamous recording session in Atlanta that almost ended in a "rumble?"), Charlie, Harold, Max, Allen, and Chris…Long-term house guests and garage – apartment dwellers: Hal, Robin, Bill's Navy Reserve buddies, Cyndi, Karen, Rachael, Dylan…

Oh, yes. Let's not forget Bill ("The Bells Are Ringing") Levy, and Rick ("I Come To The Garden Alone") Levy, to whom you were officially assigned. Remember trips to the dry cleaners, just to go behind the scenes and see how the machinery worked? The only frog in the world with a complete military wardrobe? Bill's famous Elvis impersonation at the "House of Horrors" Night Club? Tim and Ted stories? Jonathan Picrate stories (now immortalized for the next generation in the ongoing "Hazel and Jonathan" series?) Books, books, books: about Edison , Pasteur, George Washington Carver, the Curies, and several thousand others? You made learning FUN!

Piano lessons? (One who was interested; one who wasn't. THANK YOU for not forcing me!!!) Frank Boggs and the Ridgecrest choir camp? George Starke and the choir tour of the entire Western Hemisphere? One very important Fender Stratocaster guitar (you bought for me), and another equally important Fender Stratocaster guitar (we ALL chipped in to buy for Bill at Christmas; I figured the safest place to hide it from him was under his own bed…?)

Two live frogs left in a paper bag somewhere in Houston? Bill's broken leg, and how you single – handedly held everything together because Pop was out of town? Peter Pan and the boys from Never – Never Land? Walking 20 blocks (NOT 2 blocks!!) in Jacksonville to buy that part for my chemistry set? CONSTANT prayers and listening for news from Vietnam?

You taught us that EVERYTHING and EVERYBODY in life is important, and that sometimes the little things, if handled carefully, can later prove to have been more important than the big things. You taught us constancy; that whatever is worth doing is worth continuing.

You taught us that in any worthwhile project, someone usually gets stuck doing all the unappreciated, behind – the – scenes work, and you taught us not to be afraid to be that someone (you certainly have never been afraid to.)

You taught us that Love Conquers All. When we rebelled, you responded in love, not in anger. You reached out to us, and we found it impossible not to reach back.

And all of this living and teaching was aimed towards one simple yet difficult goal: to discover and live out the Will of God for our lives, even if it meant living less comfortably and doing things the hard way.

I like to think that inside every grown man and woman there still lives a memory of themselves as a child: vulnerable, selfish but longing to be taught unselfishness; a little wary of the world, yet longing to go out and change it for the better…A great, raggedy, rowdy Sunday School class of hundreds of us, waiting for the Teacher to arrive. Then the door opens, and in walks…Hassell Levy, quietly living her whole life in a way that is one simple, profound, serious, silly, inventive, childlike, adult, strong, powerful, gentle, kind, unselfish, practical, ongoing…

Sunday School lesson … and the entire class is forever changed for having had the lesson … and we love you for teaching it.

Happy birthday!! Happy Mother's Day!!

Love, Rick

Jeanette Levy Fountain – My Brother, William Earl Levy

How about getting a baby sister when you are 25 years old and married? Earl did! Born November 17, 1910, he grew up in the days of economic distress. The annual income was approximately $1,100 per year; a new car was $400-$625, and a new house was $3,200. The main element, of course was unemployment. He came from a family that was a true Leon County Florida Pioneer. Our great-great-grandfather was a settler of Tallahassee in 1827 (John McIver).

Early memories find me dancing in the arms between Earl and my older sister Myrtle and in Heaven when Earl would have me lifted up in front of him on Eagle (Earl's beautiful award-winning stallion) for "walks" around the yard. Earl's wife Hassell rode and won horse show ribbons with him at the "Trot-Away" club. Her mare was named Silver Lady.

I quickly learned to play the piano because everyone else played many instruments and mostly because I wanted to accompany Earl's singing. His love for music and his beautiful voice was a large part of my happiness in growing up.

Our mother had three brothers and four sisters. Our mother gave birth to her two boys at the same time as our grandmother had her last two children- boys! Imagine the fun and camaraderie and love each of these eleven first cousins had. They all lived close enough to walk to each other's home. Eating, sleeping, playing and praying were all shared activities! They "were" just like brothers!

Every day of our lives we "reeked" in the Baptist faith and music. Another element constantly present was self-effacing humor. Mother and Earl had a strong "case" of it - - making themselves the "brunt" of the jokes!

Earl married Hassell Williams when he was just twenty years old. He raised & provided for Hassell's two younger sisters and served as a Father figure for his niece and nephew (her sister's children). After the death of our father in 1946, he took the role of eldest son until our mother's death in 1955.

In later years Earl and I shared the desire to know "why" and "how." He and I talked so many times about our desire to research and study our interests. We called it "Locking In." When I was studying to obtain my Master's Degree at Florida State University, I knew he was in my corner because of our long talks. He also sat at my bedside at Tallahassee Memorial Hospital when I was in labor awaiting the birth of both my daughters. I named my first daughter Hassell Jeanette after Earl's wife and myself.

He truly exhibited this trait "Locking In" with the Tallahassee Fire Department exploring every facet of firefighting and equipment available throughout the United States, especially the South. He "learned" it, then "taught" it locally, at the State Fire College and Junior Colleges all over the South. He was in great demand as a speaker and teacher. We all were so very proud of him! His 38 years as Tallahassee Fire Chief demanded "his all", and he sincerely gave it.

Remember, so well, his top priority in the early days was having equipment and expertise to fight and win over fires at Elberta Crate Factory; FSU and A&M Universities. The minute the two-story buildings began to be planned/erected on the college campuses, he was focused on it.

He stayed "hip-to-hip" with Arvah Hopkins, our City Manager. He studied all plans for building and expanding the City of Tallahassee. He threw his support to being ready for the airport and its changing uses; and made sure "His Men" were capable and best at fighting this type of fire. These men knew and felt his knowledge and support for them.

My brother was a professional in all the best ways. However, his one desire (his Christian heart) was to be the kind of man who was a good enough role model to "Not" let his Brother stumble. He said to his mother so many, many times that the Lord kept this as a <u>motto</u> for <u>him</u> (Earl) loudly and clearly.

He loved to fish - HIS way! The rivers of this area provided peace and enjoyment to him. He loved the scenery and watching the water flowing by. In later years he rarely had this opportunity because he was on call at all times. Seldom did we finish a picnic, meal or any family function before he received a call and had to leave. The "Station" ruled his life, but he never resented it. He loved every aspect of it. <u>His pride was very evident with "His Men"</u>.

World War II years in Tallahassee (I was six years old) brought about loyalty and true patriotism everywhere. Those eligible volunteered (Including our cousins). Earl was told that he wasn't eligible because of the "ruling" that administrators of life-saving agencies must remain "in place". Did I mention the Levy "hard headiness'? Earl organized a plan, including the interim chief, and "Motored" to Jacksonville to enlist in the U.S. Army. My mother cried for many days thereafter, but he had made his decision. To this day I believe it was the right one for him.

His oldest child, William Earl Levy, Jr. was born January 11, 1945, during his absence. Earl was 35 years of age. He worshiped his boys; they did no wrong. We pretty much all thought so, too. Our whole family considered Rick and Bill to be our own!

It was great to see "music" in Rick and Bill for the next generations. My daddy was dying of cancer when William was born, and he dearly loved the baby whom he called "Little Earl". Rick was born April 4, 1949; graduated FSU:

PHD Psychologist; Four children; Seven grandchildren; Bill was in the Navy; graduated FSU; retired State of Florida; two daughters; and Five grandchildren.

Jeanette Levy Fountain, (presently 77 years old — December 15, 2012), MA - FSU — Retired School Teacher, Four children, Six Grandchildren and, One Great Granddaughter. Our brother O'Neal lived with me after our mother died in 1955. I had only been married one year.

Earl was energetic in his love of his Lord; family; the Fire Department; Music; Tallahassee (every aspect); Horseback Riding; fishing and his many, many friends.

His daily objective was to be honest and true. He taught the Men's Sunday School Class and was a deacon at First Baptist for many years, and our mother considered First Baptist Church as our second home.

Jeanette Levy Fountain

Appendix B

ISO Classification

Confidential   GRADING SHEET

Insurance Services Office
MUNICIPAL SURVEY SERVICE

160 Water St., New York, N.Y. 10038   230 W. Monroe St., Chicago, Ill. 60606   550 California St., San Francisco, Cal. 94104

TALLAHASSEE, FLORIDA
(See Report Dated November, 1973)

FILE NO.   POPULATION   SURVEYED

507   71,897   January, 1973

	WATER SUPPLY	FIRE DEPT.	FIRE SERV. COMM.	FIRE SAFETY CONTROL	CLIM. COND.	Divergence	TOTAL POINTS	CLASS
Points of Deficiency	407	304	42	131	32	0	916	2nd

THE CLASS OF A MUNICIPALITY IS BASED ON A TOTAL MAXIMUM OF 5000 POINTS OF DEFICIENCY AS FOLLOWS:

```
 1ST CLASS,    0 TO  500 POINTS
 2ND CLASS,  501 TO 1000
 3RD CLASS, 1001 TO 1500
 4TH CLASS, 1501 TO 2000
 5TH CLASS, 2001 TO 2500
 6TH CLASS, 2501 TO 3000
 7TH CLASS, 3001 TO 3500
 8TH CLASS, 3501 TO 4000
 9TH CLASS, 4000 TO 4500
10TH CLASS, OVER  4500
```

RELATIVE VALUES

	POINTS
WATER SUPPLY	1950
FIRE DEPARTMENT	1950
FIRE SERVICE COMMUNICATIONS	450
FIRE SAFETY CONTROL	650
	5000

ADDITIONAL POINTS OF DEFICIENCY ARE APPLIED UNDER CLIMATIC CONDITIONS WHERE THESE ARE IN EXCESS OF THE NORMAL FOR THE UNITED STATES, AND UNDER DIVERGENCE WHERE THE GRADINGS OF WATER SUPPLY AND FIRE DEPARTMENT ARE GREATLY DIFFERENT.

CONFIDENTIAL   CONFIDENTIAL

Insurance Services Office

MUNICIPAL SURVEY SERVICE

160 Water St., New York, N.Y. 10038   230 W. Monroe St., Chicago, Ill. 60606   550 California St., San Francisco, Cal. 94104

REPORT

File No. 507   on   November, 1973

TALLAHASSE, FLORIDA

GENERAL

The 1970 U.S. Census showed a population of 71,897, an increase of about 34,000 since 1955. The city covers 26.14 square miles, an increase of 14.24 square miles since the 1955 survey; about 60% of the city is closely built-upon. Elevations range from 45 to 230 feet above mean sea level. The city is in an area subject to hurricanes.

WATER SUPPLY

AN ADEQUATE SUPPLY IS AVAILABLE. PUMPING CAPACITY IS ADEQUATE BUT SLIGHTLY DEFICIENT IN RESERVE CAPACITY. PIPING ARRANGEMENTS ARE SATISFACTORY AND POWER ARRANGEMENTS ARE MAINLY GOOD. THE ARTERIAL SYSTEM IS FAIR, BEING AIDED BY THE WIDE DISTRIBUTION OF THE WELLS. THE GRIDIRON IS SOMEWHAT WIDE AND IS INCOMPLETE IN SOME SECTIONS. PRESSURES ARE FAIR TO GOOD, AND ARE WELL MAINTAINED. FIRE FLOW TESTS INDICATE THAT THE QUANTITIES AVAILABLE ARE FAIR TO GOOD IN BUSINESS DISTRICTS AND AT SHOPPING CENTERS, EXCEPT POOR AT K-MART (TEST 8); FAIRLY GOOD TO GOOD IN INDUSTRIAL DISTRICTS; MAINLY GOOD TO GOOD IN INSTITUTIONAL DISTRICTS, EXCEPT POOR AT TEST 15; AND FAIRLY GOOD TO GOOD IN RESIDENTIAL DISTRICTS.

HYDRANT SPACING IS ONLY FAIR THROUGHOUT THE CITY. HYDRANTS ARE MAINLY OF SATISFACTORY TYPE AND CONDITION IS FAIR.

*   *   *   *   *   *

General.- The system is municipally owned and operated with direct supervision of the distribution system under the superintendent of gas and water and direct supervision of water production by the superintendent of electric utilities. Civil service is not provided but long tenure is common.

Plans and records are mainly complete and up to date except plans for the Dale Mabry Supply Works are not available, and hydrant and valve records are incomplete.

It is proposed to connect the Dale Mabry Service to the Main Service and to abandon the pump station and elevated tank. It is also proposaled to strengthen the distribution system.

FIRE DEPARTMENT

THE DEPARTMENT HAS AN ADEQUATE NUMBER OF ENGINE AND LADDER COMPANIES NEEDED TO MEET THE BASIC REQUIREMENTS OF THE CITY. COMPANIES ARE MODERATELY TO CONSIDERABLY UNDERMANNED. PUMPER CAPACITY IS ADEQUATE. APPARATUS IS IN GOOD TO FAIRLY GOOD CONDITION, AND MAINLY WELL EQUIPPED. REPAIR FACILITIES ARE MAINLY GOOD AND THE PREVENTIVE MAINTENANCE PROGRAM IS SATISFACTORY. RESPONSE ASSIGNMENTS TO MOST ALARMS ARE ADEQUATE. THE TRAINING PROGRAM IS SOMEWHAT INCOMPLETE AND HAMPERED, TO SOME EXTENT BY THE LACK OF COMPLETE FACILITIES. FIRE METHODS ARE FAIRLY GOOD, BUT MAY BE ADVERSELY AFFECTED BY INADEQUATE MANNING.

☆　　　☆　　　☆　　　☆　　　☆　　　☆

Membership.- There are 113 full paid members as follows:

Fire Force:

Officers :

	Chief	8
	Company	25
Fire Fighters		65
Non-Fire Force		15

Companies.- Seven engine and 2 ladder companies are in service in 5 fire stations.

Members work an average of 56 hours per week. Considering vacations and sick leave the number normally on duty with companies is about 26. The response of off-shift members, called on second alarms, is good. A limited amount of outside aid is available but is seldom used.

Apparatus and Equipment.- Seven pumps, 2 ladder trucks, a looster truck and 2 crash trucks are in service, and 3 pumpers and a ladder truck are in reserve.

Repairs to apparatus are made at the fire department shop by a chief of maintenance and 2 mechanics. The preventive maintenance program includes annual tests of pumpers. All pumpers passed service tests, at draft, during the survey. All hose is tested annually; 40% of the 2-1/2-inch hose is over 10 years old and 26% of the 1-1/2-inch hose is over 5 years old. Hose drying facilities are provided at 2 fire stations.

Training.- Training is under the supervision of a captain and an assistant on a full-time basis. A 6-story drill tower and a pumper test pit have been built on a large hard-surfaced area behind Engine 8 quarters. Classrooms are provided at Engine 3 and Engine 8 quarters. No fire building has been provided. Extensive training, under the supervision of the training personnel, is conducted at the drill grounds, and training at stations has recently been increased to 2 hours per day. New members receive 40 hours of instruction before assignment to a company and 6 months of special instruction while on duty after assignment. No officer schools have been conducted in recent years. All members have received some training in the hazards of radioactive materials. There is a building inspection program for pre-fire planning purposes but it is inadequate in scope and frequency.

Response.- Response to box alarms and telephone alarms for fires in buildings is 2 or 3 engine companies, a ladder company and a chief officer except that a ladder company does not respond to some residential districts. A booster truck, manned by 2 members from Engine 8, responds outside the city on first alarms. During 1972 there were 1596 alarms of which 180 were for building fires and 400 alarms were from outside the city.

Operations.- Fire methods include the extensive used of booster and 1-1/2-inch hose lines. Large lines are laid by the first and subsequent arriving engine companies and pumpers are connected to hydrants when large lines are used. Connections are made to sprinkler and standpipe systems by one of the first alarm engine companies. Ventilation, ladder and salvage work are usually performed by both engine and ladder company personnel to the extent that manpower is available. Heavy and special stream appliances are used as needed, and good use is made of spray nozzles and selfcontained breathing apparatus.

Changes.- Since the 1955 report, 3 additional engine companies and one additional ladder company have been placed in service. Two additional fire stations have been constructed and 2 have been replaced. New training facilities have been provided. Department membership has been increased by 63 and although the average number of hours worked per week has been reduced by 14 the number of members on duty with companies has been considerably increased.

FIRE SERVICE COMMUNICATIONS

THE FIRE ALARM SYSTEM IS MAINLY RELIABLE AND MAINLY WELL MAINTAINED. COMMUNICATIONS CENTER EQUIPMENT IS COMPLETE AND MAINLY WELL HOUSED. BOX DISTRIBUTION IN COMMERCIAL DISTRICTS IS FAIRLY GOOD, AND ALARM CIRCUIT FACILITIES AT FIRE STATIONS ARE ADEQUATE. DEPARTMENTAL TELEPHONE FACILITIES ARE MAINLY GOOD BUT THE LISTING IN THE TELEPHONE DIRECTORY IS UNSATISFACTORY. AN ADEQUATE NUMBER OF OPERATORS ARE ON DUTY AND DISPATCHING PROCEDURES ARE GOOD.

*   *   *   *   *   *

General.- The telephone-type fire alarm system, installed in 1971, is owned and maintained by the Southeastern Telephone Company.

The communications center occupies 2 rooms on the first floor of Engine 3 quarters, 2-story building of fire resistive construction; both the rooms are properly cut off from the rest of the building. The telephone company central office through which the circuits pass is of fire-resistive construction.

Alarm System Facilities.- Communications center equipment, of manual type, is complete. Current is supplied by batteries with a common rectifier; and a manual-start generator will supply emergency power to all essential communications center equipment. Teletype and radio facilities are provided at each fire station are used as alarm circuits; all stations have an emergency generator.

There are 70 telephone-type boxes in service, all accessible to the public. The condition of paint on boxes and identifying bands on supporting poles is good.

Of the total circuit mileage 29% is in underground cable and the remainder is in messenger-supported cable.

Radio.- Base station equipment is installed in a fire station of non-combustible construction and the remot control unit is located in the communications center. Each fire apparatus has a transmitter-receiver, and 6 portable units are provided.

Telephone Facilities.- Five telephone trunk lines, of which 2 are reserved for emergency calls and arranged for progressive operation, extend to the communications center. Individual lines extend to each fire station and to various departmental offices. The listing in the telephone directory is unsatisfactory.

Operations.- One fire alarm operator is on duty at all times in the communications center. Alarms are transmitted to stations over the teletype and radio facilities.

Changes.- Since the 1955 report the fire alarm system has been replaced. This includes an increase of 27 boxes.

FIRE SAFETY CONTROL

FIRE PREVENTION

GOOD MUNICIPAL REGULATIONS HAVE BEEN ADOPTED FOR THE CONTROL OF HAZARDOUS CONDITIONS. CONTROL BY THE FIRE PREVENTION BUREAU WAS FAIR TO GOOD. MOST CONDITIONS WERE NOTED TO BE FAIR TO GOOD, WITH A FEW POOR.

*   *   *   *   *   *

Regulations.- The city has adopted the 1970 edition of the Fire Prevention Code of the American Insurance Association.

Enforcement.- Control over hazardous conditions is by the chief of the fire department assisted by a captain, a plans examiner, and 4 inspectors. The only permits issued are for above and below ground gasolene storage tanks, storage and transportation of explosives, and open burning. Inspections of hazardous occupancies are made twice a year by the fire prevention bureau. Conditions of most occupancies visited during the survey were fair to good with some poor noted in those relating to fire recapping, flammable finishes, and upholstery shops.

Good control is exercised over natural and propane gas installations.

Changes.- Fire prevention regulations have been updated and 3 additional personnel added to the fire prevention bureau.

BUILDING DEPARTMENT

BUILDING REGULATIONS ARE COMPREHENSIVE BUT ARE SOMEWHAT INADEQUATE IN SOME IMPORTANT FIRE PROTECTION FEATURES ESPECIALLY THESE RELATING TO ALLOWABLE AREAS, PROTECTION TO EXTERIOR WALL OPENINGS AND OPENINGS IN FIRE WALLS, AND THICKNESSES OF WALLS. ENFORCEMENT OF REGULATIONS APPEARS TO BE GOOD.

*   *   *   *   *   *

Regulations.- The city has adopted the 1969 edition of the Southern Standard Building Code. Some regulations have been adopted for the prevention of wind damage. Wood shingle roof covering is permitted outside the fire limits.

Enforcement.- Control over building construction is by the chief building inspector assisted by a plans examiner, a zoning technician, 3 building inspectors, 3 electrical inspectors, 4 plumbing inspectors, a director of minimum housing code enforcement, 3 housing inspectors, and 4 clerical personnel. Qualifications of personnel are good. Enforcement and procedures appears to be good. Records are complete.

Changes.- The building code has been updated and wood shingle roof coverings are now permitted. A plans examiner, a zoning technician, 2 building inspectors, 2 electrical inspectors, 3 plumbing inspectors, 4 housing personnel, and 3 clerical personnel have been added. Enforcement of regulations has improved.

ELECTRICITY

REGULATIONS AND CONTROL OVER NEW ELECTRICAL INSTALLATIONS ARE GOOD. THE GENERAL CONDITIONS OF OLDER INSTALLATIONS IS FAIR TO POOR.

*   *   *   *   *   *

Regulations.- The city has adopted the 1971 edition of the National Electrical Code.

Enforcement.- Control over electrical installations is by the chief electrical inspector assisted by 2 electrical inspectors. Qualifications are good. All wiring must be inspected prior to concealment. The power utility will not provide service without approval by the city inspector. New work is well installed. There is no established reinspection program. The general condition of older work is fair to poor. Records are good.

Changes.- The electrical code has been updated. Two additional inspectors have been appointed.

LOSS POTENTIAL ANALYSIS

SPREADING FIRES TO GROUP PROPORTIONS ARE POSSIBLE IN BUSINESS AND INDUSTRIAL DISTRICTS. ELSEWHERE FIRES SHOULD BE HELD TO THE BUILDING OF ORIGIN.

*   *   *   *   *   *

Business Districts.- The downtown business district consists of several blocks in the vicinity of Monroe and Jefferson Streets. Buildings are mainly of ordinary construction with a few of fire-resistive. Heights are mainly 1 and 2 stories with a few fire-resistive ranging up to 16 stories. A small percentage of the buildings are protected by automatic sprinklers. Other business districts extend several blocks to the north and south of the downtown district along Monroe and Adams Streets, and along Tennessee Street between Meridian and Dewey Streets and from Woodward Street to Ocala Road. Heights are generally 1 story with areas small to large. Construction is mainly ordinary. Fires should normally be held to the building or group of origin.

Shopping Centers.- The major shopping centers within the city are located along Apalachee Parkway between Goodbody Lane and Magnolin Drive (Parkway S.C.), at Thomasville and Glenview Roads (Capitol Plaza S.C.), along Apalachee Parkway at Blairstone Road (K-Mart S.C.), and at Monroe and Tharpe Streets (Northwood Mall). Construction is ordinary with areas small to large. All buildings except those at the Capitol Plaza Shopping Center are protected by automatic sprinklers. Fire lanes are normally blocked by parked automobiles. Fires at these shopping centers should be held to the building or fire area of origin.

Industrial Districts.- In the southern section of the city along the Seaboard Coast Line Railroad in an area generally bounded by Lake Bradford Road, and Madison, Boulevard, and Eugenia Streets are groups of manufacturing plants and warehouses. Construction is generally of heavy timber, ordinary and wood frame. Heights are mainly 1 or 2-stories and areas are moderate to large with the large plants protected by automatic sprinkler systems. Fires should normally be held to the building or group of origin.

Institutional Districts.- There are 3 colleges located within the city limits. Florida State University occupies about 365 acres and is generally bounded by Stadium Drive, and Tennessee, Copeland, and Jefferson Streets.

Construction is mainly fire-resistive with some ordinary interspersed. Heights range up to 12 stories with some large areas. Separation in generally good. Florida A. and M. University occupies about 367 acres and is generally bounded by Canal and Adams Streets, Orange Avenue, and Perry Street. Construction is mainly fire-resistive with some ordinary interspersed. Height range up to 4 stories with some large areas. Separation is generally good. Tallahassee Junior College occupies about 65 acres and is generally bounded by Quincy Highway, Appleyard Drive, Pensacole Street, and Blountstown Highway. Construction is generally fire-resistive. Heights are 1 or 2 stories with some areas large. Separation is good. Fire should normally be held to the building of origin.

Residential Districts.- Residential sections in the older portions of the city consist mainly of small one-story frame dwellings closely built. Newer sections consist mainly of one-story frame or brick veneer dwellings with generally good separation. The probability of a fire spreading beyond the building of origin is normally low, except in the closely-built areas.

Civil Disturbance.- There were a few minor incidents in 1968 some of which resulted in fires.

RECOMMENDED IMPROVEMENT PROGRAM

The following program has been prepared to assist the City of Tallahassee in providing better protection to life and property and may be used by the municipality as a guide for future planning. In general, recommendations under each heading are numbered in the order of their importance.

WATER SUPPLY

1. That additional hydrants be installed so that:

    a) There will be one or more at each street intersection in commercial districts depending on the required fire flow, with intermediate hydrants so that they are not over 300 feet apart.

    b) There will be one at each intersection in residential districts with intermediate hydrants so they are not over 500 feet apart.

2. That the distribution system be strengthened by the improvements necessary to provide adequate fire flows; these improvements to include the installation of the mains shown in the table, the replacement or paralleling of 4-inch mains, and the elimanation of 6-inch dead ends whenever possible. It is suggested that the following be adopted as the standard minimum size of mains for all future construction:

    a) 8 and 12-inch in commercial districts, the former to be used where it completes a good gridiron and the latter for long lines not interconnected.

b) 8-inch in residential districts; 6-inch to be used only where it completes a good gridiron, but in no case in blocks longer than 600 feet in length.

3. That all hydrants be inspected twice a year and after use at fires, the inspection to include operation at least once a year; that they be maintained in good condition; and that records be kept of inspections, operation, and condition.

4. That all hydrants installed in the future have a 4-1/2-inch and at least one 2-1/2-inch outlets with a 6-inch gated branch to at least a 6-inch main; and that a systematic program be adopted to replace 4-inch branch connections.

5a. That records be brought up to date; that duplicate copies be provided at the shop for field use and at other locations where needed; and that originals be safely filed in a fire resistive vault.

b. That all valves be inspected annually and large valves more frequently; that they be maintained in good condition; and that records be kept of inspection, operation, and condition.

FIRE DEPARTMENT

1. That at least 5 members, including an officer, be on duty at all times with each engine and ladder company.

NOTE: Six members on duty at all times with each engine and ladder company is considered standard manning.

2. That additional training facilities, including a fire building, be provided, and that the training program be expanded to include the use of the new facilities, night and multiple company drills, officer schools, and the continuation of the daily drills at fire stations; that companies make more frequent inspections of buildings for pre-fire planning purposes; and that the information be recorded on suitable forms, augmented by appropriate notes and sketches, and used as discussion material in the training program.

3. That 400 feet of 1-1/2-inch hose and 200 feet of booster hose be carried on each pumper, and that all 2-1/2-inch hose over 10 years old and all 1-1/2-inch hose over 5 years old be replaced.

4. That each pumper and ladder truck be provided with tools and appliances needed for efficient fire ground operations (See National Fire Protection Association Standard No. 19, Automotive Fire Apparatus.)

FIRE SERVICE COMMUNICATIONS

1. That additional boxes be so that one will be visible from and be within 500 feet of every building in high-valve districts, schools, nursing homes and places of public assembly.

2. That the telephone trunk lines be arranged so that the emergency lines will progress to the business lines; and that the department be property listed in the telephone directory.

FIRE SAFETY CONTROL

1. That more emphasis be placed on plan examination, inspection of new and existing installation, and maintenance of complete records so that better control can be maintained over hazardous materials, processes, and occupancies.

> NOTE: If fire company members are used to make fire prevention inspections and to enforce the fire prevention code, it is recommended that they be properly trained to handle the more common hazards and that full time bureau personnel handle the more complex hazards.

2. That the building code be amended to include those structural features necessary to provide life safety and restrict the spread of fires. It is recommended that the National Building Code of the American Insurance Association be used as a guide in framing these amendments.

3. That a complete reinspection of old wiring be made and defects corrected; and that all wiring be subsequently reinspected at suitable intervals.

Report based on survey made during January, 1973 by J.A. Speary, T.A.Tyls, amd C.E. Traficante. Acknowledgment is made of the assistance rendered by the mayor, city manager, and other officials.

Kenneth J. Carl, Director of Minicipal Surveys

TABLES

PUMPS

Station	No. of units	Capacity, each (mgd)	Pressure (psi)	Pumps from	Pumps to
Well 1	1	2.16	108	Well	Main Service
Well 2	1	2.16	117	"	" "
Well 3	1	2.37	108	"	" "
Well 4	1*	2.30	113	"	" "
Well 5	1*	2.45	115	"	" "
Well 6	1*	2.16	115	"	" "
Well 7	1*	2.16	113	"	" "
Well 8	1*	2.37	117	"	" "
Well 9	1*	2.27	130	"	" "
Well 10	1*	2.16	113	"	" "
Well 11	1*	2.16	97	"	" "
Well 12	1+	4.90	104	"	" "
Well 13	1+	4.90	110	"	" "
Dale Mabry	1	1.15	—	"	0.36-mg Clearwell
	1	1.15	—	"	" " "
	2	1.44	80	0.36-mg Clearwell	Dale Mabry Service
	2	0.58	80	0.36-mg Clearwell	Dale Mabry Service

* Standby Gasoline Engine
+ Standby Natural Gas Engine

-11-

FIRE FLOW TESTS

Test Number	Location	Service	Pressure (psi) Hydrants Closed	Quantity gpm at 20 psi Required	Quantity gpm at 20 psi Available
	BUSINESS DISTRICTS				
1	Pensacola & Monroe Sts.	M	32	5000	3000
2	Adams St. & College Ave.	M	32	5000	3100
3	Jennings & Monroe Sts.	M	82	3500	4000
4	Monroe & Brevard Sts.	M	46	2000	5800
	SHOPPING CENTERS				
5	Northwood Mall	M	38	3000	2500
6	University Plaza	M	76	2000	7100
7	Parkway	M	36	4000	2000
8	K-Mart	M	30	3000	1100
	INDUSTRIAL DISTRICTS				
9	Mabry St. & L St.	M	98	4500	2300*
10	Wahnish Way & All Saints St.	M	89	3500	6400
11	Lake Bradford Rd. & Pepper Dr.	M	96	4500	4000
	INSTITUTIONAL DISTRICTS				
12	College Ave. & Macomb St. - F.S.U.	M	65	6000	7700
13	Call & Murphree Sts. - F.S.U.	M	98	6000	5800
14	Gamble St. & Wahnish Way - F.A.M.U.	M	58	3500	3600
15	Osceola & Boulevard Sts. - F.A.M.U.	M	44	4500	2200
16	Tallahassee Jr. College - Appleyard Dr.	M	98	3000	2600
17	Jim Lee & Russell Rd. - Rickards H.S.	M	62	2000	2400
	RESIDENTIAL DISTRICTS				
18	6th St. & Crestview Ave.	M	41	1500	4900
19	Lemond St & Randolph Circle	M	49	1000	2700
20	10th Ave. & Branch St.	M	49	1500	3200
21	Thomasville Rd. & 6th Ave.	M	38	2000	2900
22	4th Ave. & Bainbridge Rd.	M	81	2000	10800
23	Pope & Brevard St.	M	88	2000	5600
24	Park Ave & Satsuma St.	M	31	1500	1200
25	Circle & Old Fort Drs.	M	36	1500	2300

-12-

FIRE FLOW TESTS

Test Number	Location	Service	Pressure (psi) Hydrants Closed	Quantity gpm at 20 psi Required	Quantity gpm at 20 psi Available
	RESIDENTIAL DISTRICTS (Cont'd).				
26	Nininger & Wainwright	DM	51	1500	3000
27	Holton St. bet. Orange Ave. & Weis St.	M	90	2000	1700
28	Holokin near Nene & Chuli Nene	M	53	1000	1500
29	Lothian & Lasswade Dr.	M	46	1000	3200
30	Myrick Rd. & Rhonda Dr.	M	71	1500	4700
	OUTSIDE THE CITY				
31	Tallahasse Mall	M	63	5000	3300

M = Main Service
DM = Dale-Mabry Service
* Additional Quantity Available from Dale-Mabry Service

RECOMMENDED MAINS

Size (Inches)	Along	From	To
16	Stuckey St.	Indian River St.	Lake Bradford Rd.
12	US 90	Appleyard Dr.	McKeithan St.
12*	Lake Bradford Rd., Seminole Dr. & S. Augustine St.		
12*	Adams & Jefferson Sts.	Call St.	Monroe St.
12*	Lake Bradford Rd. & Kissimmee St.	Stuckey St.	Waknish Way
8	Orange Ave.	Munson	Holton St.
8	Indian Head Dr.	Apalachee Pkwy.	Lafayette St.
8	Pensacola St.	Appleyard Dr.	Cactus St.
8	Herty St.	Pensacola St.	Existing 6"
8	Chipley St.	Jackson Bluff Rd.	Plant St.

* Proposed

-14-

FIRE COMPANIES AND APPARATUS

Company	Location	Members Normally on Duty	Apparatus Type and Year Built
Eng. 3	S. Adams St. Bet. Virginia & Tennessee Sts.	4	1000-gpm Pumper-1967
Eng. 5	Sixth Ave. near Monroe St.	2	1000-gpm Pumper-1965
Eng. 7	Tallahassee Municipal Airport	3	600-gpm Pumper-1957 Crash Tk.-1955 Crash Tk.-1951
Eng. 8	Pensacola St. and Appleyard Dr.	3	750-gpm Pumper-1968 Booster Tk.-1943*
Eng. 11	With Engine 5	2	750-gpm Pumper-1963
Eng. 12	Monroe St. and Magnolia Dr.	3	750-gpm Pumper-1963
Eng. 22	With Engine 3	3	750-gpm Pumper-1970
Lad. 1	With Engine 3	3	85-Ft. Elev. Plat. Tk.-1972
Lad. 4	With Engine 12	3	100-Ft. Aer. Lad. Tk.-1965

* Manned by members of Engine 8 when response is made outside of the city.

NOTE: Three Pumpers and one Aerial Ladder Truck in reserve.

FIRE PROTECTION MAP

    Black and white prints of the Fire Protection Map made in connection with the survey of Tallahassee are available upon request to city officials and insurance companies receiving this report at a cost of $4.50 each, postpaid. This map is 42 inches by 56 inches and shows water mains, fire flow test locations, and fire company locations. Orders for prints should be sent to:

        Municipal Survey Service
        Insurance Services Office
        160 Water Street
        New York, New York 10038

Appendix C

Congressional Record and Resolutions

City of Tallahassee Proclamation – May 5, 1970

Leon County Board of Commissioners Resolution - May 4, 1970

State of Florida Senate Resolution – May 7, 1970

State of Florida Senate Resolution – April 28, 1976

Congressional Record — Extensions of Remarks – March 29, 1977

Letter from Congressman Don Fuqua to Chief Levy re:
Congressional Record Entry – March 31, 1977

Florida Fire Chiefs Association – Resolution upon Chief Levy's Passing – 1986

P R O C L A M A T I O N

WHEREAS, Earl Levy became employed by the City of Tallahassee Fire Department in 1927 at the age of 16, and,

WHEREAS, he worked his way up through the ranks and was appointed Chief on May 1, 1940, and,

WHEREAS, during his tenure as Chief the department has grown from 1 station and 9 men to 5 stations and 104 employees, and,

WHEREAS, the citizens enjoy one of the most favorable fire insurance ratings of any comparable city in America as a result of an effective Fire Prevention Program, and,

WHEREAS, Earl Levy exemplifies the highest in professional competency, dedication to duty and selfless service to the public,

NOW, THEREFORE, by virtue of the authority vested in me as Mayor of the City of Tallahassee, I proclaim Tuesday, May 5, 1970

"EARL LEVY DAY"

LEE A. EVERHART, MAYOR-COMMISSIONER

ATTEST:

LOUIS H. COOK, CITY AUDITOR AND CLERK

RESOLUTION

WHEREAS, it has come to the attention of the Board of County Commissioners of Leon County, Florida, that there is planned for May 5, 1970, a ceremony honoring Earl Levy for his thirty years of untiring and dedicated service to the citizens of Leon County as the Chief of the Fire Department of the City of Tallahassee, and

WHEREAS, the said Earl Levy has dedicated his life to the efficiency of the operation of the said fire department to such an extent that this area ranks among the highest in the nation in the protection afforded by a municipal fire department, and

WHEREAS, the said Earl Levy has not only been concerned with the efficiency of such department but also with the caliber and morale of the employees of such department to the extent that his dedication to duty has set for them an example which is inspiring to all;

NOW, THEREFORE, BE IT RESOLVED, by the Board of County Commissioners of Leon County, Florida, in special meeting assembled this 4th day of May, A. D. 1970, that in behalf of the citizens of Leon County, that the said Earl Levy, Chief of the Fire Department of the City of Tallahassee, be and he is hereby highly commended for the thirty years of dedicated, efficient and effective service which he has performed, and the hope is expressed that the said Earl Levy will continue to serve in the future so as to provide the citizens of Leon County, Florida, with the same outstanding protection that his leadership has provided in the past.

STATE OF FLORIDA

COUNTY OF LEON

I, PAUL F. HARTSFIELD, Clerk of the Circuit Court in and for Leon County, Florida, and ex-officio Clerk of the Board of County Commissioners of Leon County, Florida, hereby certify that the above and foregoing is a true and correct copy of a resolution adopted by the Board of County Commissioners of Leon County, Florida, in Special Meeting assembled this 4th day of May, A. D. 1970, and that the same has been duly recorded in the Minutes of said Board.

IN WITNESS WHEREOF, I have hereunto affixed my hand and official seal this 4th day of May, A. D. 1970.

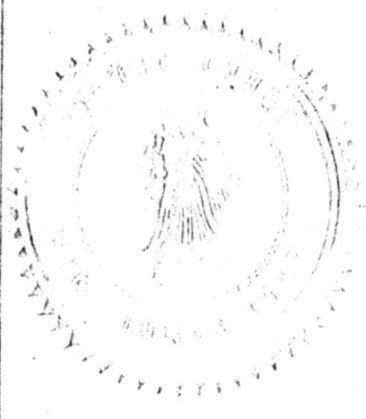

/s/ Paul F. Hartsfield
Clerk, Board of County Commissioners, Leon County, Florida

By: C. A. Turner
C. A. Turner, Deputy Clerk

May 7, 1970

...REAS, the people of the State of Florida have long ...pride in the athletic efforts and accomplishments of ...representing the state, and

...REAS, the Jacksonville University basketball team did ...an exemplary exhibit of talent, dedication, and courage ...an unprecedented pinnacle of achievement by being the ...Florida school to reach the National Collegiate Athletic ...tion basketball finals and in so doing did receive the ... national ranking ever afforded a team from the State of ..., and

...REAS, by their efforts the Jacksonville University ...ball team has brought honor and recognition to the State ...ida and the citizens thereof, and

...REAS, the people of the great State of Florida recognize ...xtraordinary skill, effort and dedication required of all ...associated with the Jacksonville University Athletic ... which has produced a basketball team of such ...ment,

Therefore, Be It Resolved by the Senate of the State of ...ida:

...the Senate of the State of Florida in regular session ...led, does hereby congratulate Jacksonville University and ...ketball team for its accomplishments and the honor and ...nition brought unto the State of Florida by the efforts of ...Jacksonville University Basketball team during the ...1970 basketball season, and orders that an engrossed copy ...is resolution, bearing the signatures of the elected leaders ... Senate of the State of Florida be presented unto Dr. ...rt Harry Spiro, President, Jacksonville University.

...s taken up and read the second time in full. On motion by ...or Beaufort, SR 1351 was adopted and certified to the ... The vote was: Yeas—41 Nays—None

...resident	de la Parte	McClain	Slade
...	Ducker	Myers	Stolzenburg
...s	Friday	Ott	Stone
...n	Gong	Plante	Thomas
...fort	Gunter	Pope	Trask
	Henderson	Poston	Williams
...	Hollahan	Reuter	Wilson
...on	Horne	Saunders	Young
	Johnson	Sayler	
...	Karl	Scarborough	
	Knopke	Shevin	

...1373—A resolution commending Earl Levy of Tallahas... Leon County, for meritorious and outstanding service to ...ate and community.

...EREAS, Earl Levy began employment with the Tallahas...ire Department on March 15, 1927 at the age of sixteen,

...EREAS, Earl Levy was appointed chief of the Tallahassee ...Department May 1, 1940, at age twenty-nine, and

...EREAS, Chief Levy was a member of the first Board of ...ees of the Florida State Fire College, and

...EREAS, Chief Levy served on the Board of Directors of ...lorida State Firemen's Association, and

...EREAS, Chief Levy was a member of the two-man ...ittee which wrote the bylaws establishing the present ...a Association of Fire Chiefs, and

...EREAS, Chief Levy served as Chaplain of the Florida ...ation of Fire Chiefs, and

...REAS, Chief Levy served as President of the Florida ...e Chiefs Association and

...REAS, Chief Levy served as President of the Southeast...ivision of the International Association of Fire Chiefs, and

...REAS, Chief Levy appeared on the program of the ...National Fire Department Instructors Conference, and

...EREAS, Chief Levy as a graduate in Municipal Fire ...stration from the Institute for Training in Municipal ...istration, and

WHEREAS, Chief Levy has been an instructor in fire department administration at the Florida Fire College, and

WHEREAS, Chief Levy has served as Chairman of the Education Committee of the State Fire Chiefs, and

WHEREAS, Chief Levy has served extensively as a member of special committees formulated by the late W. Fred Heister of Oklahoma State University for the purpose of providing and reviewing material embodied in the Fire Service Training Manuals of the International Fire Service Training Association, and

WHEREAS, Chief Levy served as liaison representative for the State Fire Chiefs Association in meetings of the United States Forest Service and all Florida fire service organizations for reviewing the development of an Example Type of Fire Defense Plan for Civil Defense in Florida, and

WHEREAS, Chief Levy is a past recipient of the Tallahassee Junior Chamber of Commerce Good Government Award, the Cooper-Taylor Memorial Award for public safety, promotion from the Florida Junior Chamber of Commerce; Woodmen of the World Award for community service; and the Distinguished Service Award from the state fire marshal, and

WHEREAS, Chief Levy is a Deacon of his Church; a member of the Kiwanis Club, Elks Club, Odd Fellows, Florida State Firemen's Association, Florida Fire Chiefs Association, and International Fire Service Training Association, NOW, THEREFORE,

Be It Resolved by the Senate of the State of Florida:

That the Senate of the State of Florida does hereby recognize and show its appreciation to Chief Earl Levy of Tallahassee, Florida for the devotion and service he has shown the State of Florida.

BE IT FURTHER RESOLVED that Chief Earl Levy be presented a copy of this resolution, with the signature of the President affixed, as testament to the action herein taken by the Senate of the State of Florida.

Was taken up and read the second time in full. On motion by Senator Horne, SR 1373 was adopted and certified to the House. The vote was: Yeas—41 Nays—None

Mr. President	de la Parte	McClain	Slade
Askew	Ducker	Myers	Stolzenburg
Bafalis	Friday	Ott	Stone
Barron	Gong	Plante	Thomas
Beaufort	Gunter	Pope	Trask
Bell	Henderson	Poston	Williams
Boyd	Hollahan	Reuter	Wilson
Broxson	Horne	Saunders	Young
Chiles	Johnson	Sayler	
Daniel	Karl	Scarborough	
Deeb	Knopke	Shevin	

Consideration of SCR 1379 was deferred, the bill retaining its place on the Calendar.

SCR 784—A concurrent resolution designating Interstate Highway 95 from Miami to the Georgia state line as the Dwight David Eisenhower Memorial Highway.

WHEREAS, the administration of Dwight David Eisenhower marked the beginning of the interstate highway system throughout this great nation, and

WHEREAS, due to the beginnings of this effort, Florida and the nation now have a highway system undreamed of at the turn of this century, and

WHEREAS, in naming Interstate Highway 95 for the late Dwight David Eisenhower, 35th President of the United States of America, the citizens of this state and the nation will be reminded of his leadership as Supreme Allied Commander of the forces which defeated Nazi Germany in World War II, NOW, THEREFORE,

Be It Resolved by the Senate of the State of Florida, the House of Representatives Concurring:

That out of gratitude for his leadership in war and peace and in recognition of Dwight David Eisenhower's contribution to this state, this nation, and this world, Interstate Highway 95 is

By Senators P. Thomas and Barron

A Resolution commending the Tallahassee Fire Department and its Chief, William Earl Levy, Sr.

WHEREAS, the City of Tallahassee has received an overall Class 2 insurance rating from the Insurance Services Office as a result of field surveys performed throughout the nation, and this is mainly attributable to the efficiency of the Tallahassee Fire Department under the direction of William Earl Levy, Sr., who first became employed as a paid member of the fire department when a youth of 16, and who took command of the fire department in 1940 when the city had only a Class 6 insurance rating, and

WHEREAS, no other city in Florida has a Class 2 insurance rating, an achievement which has been attained by only 38 cities in the United States, no city having ever been awarded the higher Class 1 rating, and

WHEREAS, the caliber and compassion of the firemen and the proficiency of the Tallahassee Fire Department under the able direction of Chief Levy was exemplified by the expert manner in which it safely evacuated all of the elderly residents from the twelve-story Georgia Belle Dickinson Apartments, expeditiously extinguished the fire without loss of life or serious injury, and afterward humbly knelt to thank God for His assistance, and

WHEREAS, the citizens of Tallahassee respect and appreciate their Fire Department for its ability to arrive at the scene of a fire with care and utmost speed, its skill in extinguishing a fire with minimum damage and disturbance to other areas, its customary precaution of returning to the premises to determine if it is secure, and the many acts of human kindness performed by Chief Levy and his staff that create a calming influence on those unfortunate ones who experience the tragedy of watching their life's possessions being consumed by flames, and

WHEREAS, the Tallahassee Fire Department, composed of meticulously selected personnel, expertly trained, and instilled with pride and compassion by Chief Levy who is totally dedicated to constant improving and upgrading of firefighting techniques, inspections, and training programs, has made the Department probably the most superb service agency in the area and has set an example for all Florida fire departments, NOW, THEREFORE,

Be It Resolved by the Senate of the State of Florida:

That the Tallahassee Fire Department and its Chief, William Earl Levy, Sr., are hereby commended for their efficiency in fire prevention and control which has helped earn the City of Tallahassee an overall Class 2 insurance rating from the Insurance Services Office, a rating to be emulated by every city of this state.

BE IT FURTHER RESOLVED that copies of this resolution, signed by the President of the Senate and duly attested by the Secretary, be transmitted to the Tallahassee Fire Department and to its Chief, William Earl Levy, Sr., as tangible tokens of the gratitude and respect of the Florida Senate.

This is a true and correct copy of Senate Resolution No. 1190, adopted by The Florida Senate on April 28, 1976.

Dempsey J. Barron
President of the Senate

FIREMAN'S FIREMAN: CHIEF EARL LEVY

HON. DON FUQUA
OF FLORIDA
IN THE HOUSE OF REPRESENTATIVES

Tuesday, March 29, 1977

Mr. FUQUA. Mr. Speaker, the image of the fireman is deeply embedded in the hearts and minds of the American people. Every child has been excited at the sound of the siren, the flashing lights, and the bright red trucks speeding to answer an alarm.

That scene masks a very serious and dangerous occupation, one in which many have lost their lives serving others.

One of the finest men ever to serve the profession has completed 50 years of service as a fireman with the Tallahassee, Fla., Fire Department. He is Earl Levy, the chief of that department, and one who is respected in and out of the profession.

A tribute which says it all was published recently in an editorial in the Tallahassee Democrat, the newspaper serving my State's capital city. As a tribute to this remarkable gentleman, and his profession, I ask that it be printed in the pages of this journal for others to share:

Fire Chief Earl Levy began his 51st year as a Tallahassee fireman today. Tuesday he celebrated his conclusion of 50 years of service, a truly remarkable accomplishment.

It was March 15, 1927 that Levy, a youth of 16 years, began work with the fire department. He advanced through the ranks and on May 1, 1940 was appointed chief of a department which had nine men and one station. Today there are more than 100 in the department working out of five stations.

During the past half a century Levy has displayed not only a devotion to duty, but a devotion to improving the capabilities of the fire department and of the men who work for it. As a result of his efforts Tallahassee enjoys the best fire insurance rating of any city in the Southeast.

A constant training program is carried out within the department. Firemen study the latest techniques and also become familiar with those buildings to which they might be called.

Many honors have come to Levy over the years and he has served with many organizations interested in fire safety.

He has served as president of the Southeastern Division of the International Association of Fire Chiefs. He has appeared on programs of the National Fire Department Instructors Conference and served as chairman of the Educational Committee of State Fire Chiefs when that committee was instrumental in getting firefighting service courses, leading to an associate degree, accepted on the college level.

Seven years ago, on the anniversary of his 30 years as chief, Levy was honored with a dinner and with special resolutions adopted by both houses of the Florida Legislature and the Cabinet.

Levy's golden anniversary as a fireman was quiet. City Commissioners adopted a resolution honoring him at last night's meeting. For Chief, however, it was another work day, one more since he had joined the department 18,263 days ago. We hope he will have many more.

In the most honorable sense of the word, Chief Levy has been a public servant. We congratulate him for it. Tallahassee is rightfully proud and thankful for his service.

CONGRATULATIONS CHIEF

DON FUQUA
2D DISTRICT
FLORIDA

2266 RAYBURN HOUSE OFFICE BUILDING
WASHINGTON, D.C. 20515

CONGRESS OF THE UNITED STATES
HOUSE OF REPRESENTATIVES
WASHINGTON, D.C. 20515

March 31, 1977

Honorable Earl Levy
Chief
Tallahassee Fire Department
327 N. Adams Street
Tallahassee, Florida 32301

Dear Chief Levy:

The enclosed tribute which appeared in the Congressional Record is a tribute to a remarkable record and a distinguished gentleman.

Your ability, service and integrity are recognized wherever your profession gathers and I wanted to join all of those who know of that record in paying tribute to a record without equal.

You have my sincere best wishes and congratulations.

Sincerely,

DON FUQUA
Member of Congress

DF/Wcg
Enclosure

FLORIDA FIRE CHIEF'S ASSN.

1986

RESOLUTION   1

WHEREAS, the Florida Fire Chiefs Association has at the opening session of its 29th Annual Conference, held in Dade County, Florida, July 20-23 1986, paused to remember our Brother Chiefs that have passed from this life during the past year, AND,

WHEREAS, the Florida Fire Chiefs Association has recognized these members for their untiring efforts on our behalf and on behalf of their communities by helping to preserve life and property, AND,

WHEREAS, the names of Chief William C. Wolf (Winter Haven), Chief William Gunther (Ocean-Broward County), Chief William Earl Levy, Sr. (Tallahassee), Chief James Talmage Vandergrift (Ocoee), Chief William F. O'Brien (Palm Beach Gardens), Chief George Robert Kennedy, Sr. (Edgewater), Chief Paul F. Walls (Edgewater), and Chief A.L. Bedenbaugh (Ocala) are permanently etched in our memory due to their good deeds in the name of the Fire Service.

THEREFORE BE IT RESOLVED, that the Florida Fire Chiefs Association expresses its deepest sympathy and sorrow to the families of Chief William C. Wolf, Chiefs William Gunther, Chief William Earl Levy, Chief James Talmage Vandergrift, Chief William F. O'Brien, Chief George Robert Kennedy, Sr., Chief Paul F. Walls and Chief A.L. Bedenbaugh.

The membership of the Florida Fire Chiefs Association further RESOLVES to rededicate ourselves to the job that remains undone, to further the professionalism of our association and to maintain the high standards and ideals that have been set by those who have answered their last alarm.

Appendix D

Letters

- Letter from Chief Levy to Chief George McDaniel - June 30, 1971

- Letter from R. W. Carter to Chief Levy - August 17, 1973

- Letter from Delmar Publishers requesting Chief Levy write a college-level text book - January 16, 1974

- Letter from Ralph E. Proctor Sr. - January 28, 1975

- Letter from Chief Levy to Ralph E. Proctor Sr. - February 20, 1975

- Letter from Chief Levy to Assistant Chief Clyde Johnson - September 20, 1956

- Letter from Chief Levy to Deputy Chief Morris Wainwright - September 30, 1966

- Letter from Chief Levy to Deputy Chief James Cureton - March 31, 1977

- Letter from Chief Levy to Captain Fred Mitchell - August 15, 1975

- Retirement Request from Chief Levy to City Manager, Daniel A. Kleman - November 30, 1977

- Letter from Chief Levy to Maryland State Fire Marshal, James C. Robertson – March 9, 1979

- Letter from City Manager, Daniel A. Kleman to Chief Levy - September 28, 1978

GENE BERKOWITZ
MAYOR COMMISSIONER

SPURGEON CAMP
MAYOR PRO-TEM COMMISSIONER

LEE A. EVERHART
COMMISSIONER

JAMES R. FORD
COMMISSIONER

LORING LOVELL
COMMISSIONER

ARVAH B. HOPKINS
CITY MANAGER

LOUIS H. COOK
CITY AUDITOR-CLERK

ROY T. RHODES
CITY ATTORNEY

HAYWARD V. ATKINSON
ASS'T. CITY ATTORNEY

HARRY H. MITCHELL
MUNICIPAL JUDGE

EDW. J. HILL
CITY SOLICITOR

June 30, 1971

Mr. George L. McDaniel
Assistant Chief
Tallahassee Fire Department
Tallahassee, Florida

Dear Chief "Mac":

As I write this letter, I do so with mixed emotions. You have given many years of faithful and dedicated service to the fire department of the City of Tallahassee. You have earned the privilege of having many happy years of retirement and relaxation. All of us in the fire department wish God's richest blessings on you and your wife.

I will personally miss you very much in your professional capacity and more than you can ever know as a personal friend. You may rest assured that you have contributed much towards making the Tallahassee fire department what it is today.

Please do not neglect to come by to see us anytime you can. You will always be an assistant chief in this department. As a final thing, I am hereby appointing you as an <u>honorary lifetime assistant chief</u>. You will eventually receive a badge designating such, but it was impossible to have that for today.

May you meet with success in all of your future undertakings.

Sincerely,

Earl Levy, Chief
Fire Department
Tallahassee, Florida

el:mj

"FLORIDA'S CAPITAL CITY" SERVING ALL FLORIDA

JOAN R. HEGGEN
MAYOR-COMMISSIONER

JAMES R. FORD
MAYOR PRO TEM-COMMISSIONER

RUSSELL R. BEVIS
COMMISSIONER

SPURGEON CAMP
COMMISSIONER

EARL L. YANCEY
COMMISSIONER

ARVAH B. HOPKINS
CITY MANAGER

LOUIS H. COOK
CITY AUDITOR-CLERK

BRYAN W. HENRY
CITY ATTORNEY

EDW. J. HILL
CITY SOLICITOR

17 August 1973

Chief Earl Levy
327 North Adams Street
Tallahassee, Florida

Dear Chief:

I wanted to write you a brief note and thank you for the wonderful professional experience and companionship which I encountered on our in-service tour which we recently made in the cities of St. Petersburg and Lakeland.

This trip was most rewarding to me and has given me a great deal of insight into what other personnel areas are doing. I especially enjoyed the wholesome, positive attitudes that you have concerning your fellow man, fellow workers and your overall expertise in the area of Fire Fighting, Safety, Management and Personnel relations.

You are undoubtly one of the most learned men in the area of human relations that I have had the pleasure of knowing.

Rest assured, that because I know of your abilities and potentials, I intend to ask you many pertinent facts related to overall personnel operations of this great City of Tallahassee, and knowing you as the kind of person you are, I know you will extend to me all the time that you have available.

Again, thank you for the tremendous time and fellowship shared in our recent trip and my very best wishes to you as you continue rending your most capable services as Fire Chief for the City of Tallahassee.

Cordially,

R. W. Carter

RWC/h

"FLORIDA'S CAPITAL CITY" — SERVING ALL FLORIDA

delmar publishers

P.O. BOX 5087
ALBANY, NEW YORK 12205
PHONE 518-459-1150

January 16, 1974

Career Education Consulting Editors:

Allied Health
 B. Atkinson

Practical Nursing
 L. Broadwell

Registered Nursing
 B. Dean

Home Economics
 E. Caldwell

Early Childhood
 J. Machado

Data Processing
 E. Marxer

Management
 R. Moran

Marketing
 G. Schornack

Electronic Technology
 R. Castellucis

Mechanical Technology
 N. Abell

Electromechanical
 R. Tinnell

Fire Science
 D. Favreau

Law Enforcement
 K. McCreedy

Masonry/Building
 R. Kreh

Industrial Arts
 A. Kaumeheiwa

Cosmetology
 A. McCarthy

Career Specialist
 H. Sinnamon

Mr. Earl Levy
109 S. Adams St.
Tallahassee, FL 32301

Dear Mr. Levy:

    Would you or one of your associates be interested in writing a textbook aimed at the two-year college market? We are now publishing for this level and are seeking talent to write our materials.

    The curriculum development department has completed the preliminary work on the fire science textbooks and I'd like to send you additional information if you so desire.

    If you find it more convenient, feel free to write some brief comments on the bottom of this letter and return it in the enclosed self-addressed envelope.

Sincerely,

Mary Grauerholz
Acquisition Editor

MG
Enc.

A DIVISION OF LITTON EDUCATIONAL PUBLISHING, INC. ● LITTON INDUSTRIES

Barnett Bank of Tallahassee

IOPK INS
kGER
DOK
TOR·CLERK
I EN RY

Calhoun at Jefferson
P. O. Box 870
Tallahassee, Florida 32302 Telephone: (904) 224-1111

January 28, 1975

Mr. Earl Levy
543 East 8th Avenue
Tallahassee, Florida   32303

Dear Chief:

Since our friendship and association in the Fire Department of the City of Tallahassee goes back <u>many many</u> years to the time of the Volunteer Department days, it is with great personal pleasure that I note your latest award as the "Outstanding Public Administrator of 1974."

My sincere congratulations on the above award and for the outstanding job you have been and are doing for all of us in Tallahassee.

I hope that we will both be around for quite a few more years for us to enjoy our friendship.

Sincerely,

Ralph E. Proctor, Sr.

REP:lc

JOAN R HEGGEN
MAYOR-COMMISSIONER

JAMES R. FORD
MAYOR PRO TEM-COMMISSIONER

RUSSELL R. BEVIS
COMMISSIONER

LORING LOVELL
COMMISSIONER

ARVAH B. FIO
CITY MANAG

LOUIS H. CO
CITY AUDITO

BRYAN W. HEN
CITY ATTORN

LOW. J. HILL.
L.CY SOLICIT

February 20, 1975

Mr. Ralph E. Proctor, Sr.
P. O. Box 880
Tallahassee, Florida

Dear Ralph:

Our friendship does indeed date back many years, and you and I have seen a great deal of change since the days of the Volunteer department. All of this makes me particularly grateful for your nice letter.

I am <u>ever</u> conscious of the early day contributions of the old Volunteer department. The support of its members has been very far reaching down through the years.

Thank you for the kind words and congratulations. However, I honestly feel that credit for any success we enjoy must be shared with many others, some of whom are no longer with us.

Sincerely,

Forever your friend,

September 20, 1956
Mr. C. D. Johnson
Third Assistant Chief
Fire Department
City of Tallahassee
Dear Clyde:
I am entirely in sympathy with your motives in requesting retirement from the Fire Department. However, the department will suffer a great loss, and I personally will feel definitely that you are leaving a gap which will be very difficult to fill. Not only does this feeling exist in regard to your work in the Fire Department, but also as a very close personal friend.
I wish you many years of good health and happiness in connection with your every undertaking.
Sincerely,

Earl Levy, Chief
Fire Department
Tallahassee, Florida

GEORGE S. TAFF
MAYOR-COMMISSIONER
J. W. CORDELL
MAYOR PRO TEM-COMMISSIONER
DAVIS H. ATKINSON
COMMISSIONER
WILLIAM H. CATES
COMMISSIONER
HUGH E. WILLIAMS JR.
COMMISSIONER

ARVAH B. HOPKINS
CITY MANAGER
LOUIS H. COOK
CITY AUDITOR-CLERK
ROY T. RHODES
CITY ATTORNEY
RIVERS BUFORD, JR
ASS'T CITY ATTORNEY
EDGAR C. BOOTH
MUNICIPAL JUDGE
EDW J. HILL
CITY SOLICITOR

September 30, 1966

Mr. Morris Wainright
Deputy Chief, Fire Department
City of Tallahassee
Tallahassee, Florida

Dear Sir:

I wish for you upon this occasion of your retirement the best of everything in your future undertakings.

We will miss you very much in the Tallahassee Fire Department. You have been the most able and faithful deputy chief that I have ever seen. You feel more like a brother to me than a business associate.

I do not want anybody else ever to wear your deputy chief's badge. It was the first badge ever bought for this rank in the Tallahassee Fire Department. On behalf of the City, I am hereby presenting it to you.

Further, it is the desire of every one in the department that you never forget your association with it. With this thought in mind I am bestowing on you the first life-time honorary deputy chief's rank in this department. Such a badge will be ordered for you in addition to your own in order that you may have them both always.

Sincerely,

Earl Levy
Chief, Fire Department
City of Tallahassee
Tallahassee, Florida

el:mj

"FLORIDA'S CAPITAL CITY" — SERVING ALL FLORIDA

March 31, 1977

Mr. James H. Cureton, Deputy Chief
Tallahassee Fire Department
Tallahassee, Florida

Dear Chief Cureton:

I realize I have already told you, probably several times, how much I appreciated the fiftieth anniversary cake.

However, I wish to tell you again, on paper, just what it meant to me, and if there were others involved in this matter, please convey my thanks to them.

You are not only my second in command, but very probably my best friend on this earth. I feel this cake was evidence of a very far reaching and strong bond between us. As you know, I am a pretty sentimental sort of person and continually have to strive very hard to keep from showing evidence of this fact.

You may know that this particular occasion really got to me.

You are highly efficient in your capacity as Deputy Chief, and no man could ask for more in the way of job loyalty, dedication, personal loyalty, and professionalism than you have displayed. My personal admiration for you knows no bounds.

May the Good Lord bless you and your entire family.

Sincerely,

Earl Levy, Chief
Tallahassee Fire Department
Tallahassee, Florida

el:mj

JOHN R. JONES
MAYOR-COMMISSIONER
DONALD C. PRICE
MAYOR PRO TEM-COMMISSIONER
JAMES R. FORD
COMMISSIONER
BEN W. THOMPSON, JR.
COMMISSIONER
EARL L. YANCEY
COMMISSIONER

DANIEL A. KLEMAN
CITY MANAGER
HERBERT J. SECKEL
CITY AUDITOR-CLERK
BRYAN W. HENRY
CITY ATTORNEY
EDW. J. HILL
CITY SOLICITOR

CITY HALL
32304

August 15, 1975

Mr. Fred L. Mitchell, Captain
Tallahassee Fire Department
Tallahassee, Florida

Dear Sir:

Your request for retirement from the fire department has been properly processed and approved.

We all hold you in very high regard, and you have rendered invaluable service to this department.

You were on the eligibility list for the next appointment to assistant chief, and unfortunately, you were not able to assume this active position.

Therefore, as you retire, you are hereby appointed as an assistant chief in the Tallahassee Fire Department, and your retirement plaque is given to Assistant Chief Fred L. Mitchell.

Yours truly,

Earl Levy

Earl Levy, Chief
Tallahassee Fire Department
Tallahassee, Florida

el mj

November 30, 1977

Mr. Daniel A.
Kleman City Manager

Tallahassee, Florida

Dear Sir:

As you <u>know,</u> I have, for the past two or three years, from time to time given serious thought to an actual date for my retirement from the fire department. For the past year <u>specifically,</u> you have known that I would probably choose the end of 1977.

Such a date has now become clearly fixed in my mind, and I know there is a season for all things. I might point out that this month marked my sixty-seventh birthday. Such an age makes it impossible to plan ongoing programs and execute them for future desirable effects and fairness to the City.

I have served with many wonderful people in our department, some of whom have actually passed on. My lifetime career has constituted a source of great reward and comfort to me for over fifty years. It is my conviction that the department has reached a very high level of efficiency and development. Such will be maintained only through the efforts of present and future personnel and the cooperation of the community. There are today many very fine men in this department, and they are quite capable of maintaining the present level of service rendered to the public.

No fire chief could have had better deputy chiefs than I have had down through the years. They were, of course, Deputy Chief Morris Wainright (retired), Deputy Chief Ed Wynn (deceased), and Deputy Chief James Cureton now retiring. Any one of them could have been a wonderful overall chief for this city. We have an outstanding group of assistant chiefs, captains, lieutenants, and total personnel. The administrative staff is very loyal, efficient, and dedicated.

Page 2 - Mr. Kleman - November 30, 1977

Down through the years, I have received outstanding cooperation from all City officials elected and appointed. This applies also to all employees and other department heads.

My personal relationship with <u>you</u> has been very close and pleasant, indeed, and it is most unusual considering the vast difference in our ages. May the Good Lord bless you and your family in all things.

It is my desire that you will grant my request for retirement January 15, 1978.

Yours truly,

[signature: Levy Sr.]

William Earl Levy,
Sr. Chief, Fire Department 327 North Adams Street
Tallahassee, Florida

wel:mj

543 East 8th Avenue
Tallahassee, Florida
March 9, 1979

Mr. James C. Robertson,
Fire Marshal State Office Building
301 West Preston Street
Baltimore, Maryland 21201

Dear "Robbie":

It is a real pleasure to receive your nice letter. Down through the years I have regarded you as one of my <u>very best</u> friends.

Your career has been most interesting to me and you developed in a marvelous fashion. My mind goes back to some of our talks in the very early days. I remember so *very* vividly one night in the old Tallahassee Headquarters station when we talked into the wee small hours of the morning.

It would have been very nice, and I would have been proud, if you could have been present at my retirement party. The Florida State University Ogilvie Ballroom had over 600 people. I was told that this was their greatest number ever for a retirement banquet. Many State, County and City officials, rich and poor were present with Judges, Lawyers and representatives of every segment of Tallahassee's total Community. In addition, there were many out of town fire service folks.

Honestly, I had occasionally wondered down through the years just what it would be like to retire. I had sometimes thought that it would be better to just slip quietly away, but that was not to be.

No man could ever have a more <u>rewarding</u> career than I had, and it was wonderful to know that even with my 67 years of

age our young 31 year old city manager shed tears when I left. Also, he did as I asked him to and appointed the man I wanted as Chief.
I will be looking forward to seeing you
again. Your friend,

Earl

Earl Levy

NEAL D. SAPP
MAYOR-COMMISSIONER

SHELDON E. HILAMAN
MAYOR PRO TEM-COMMISSIONER

JAMES R. FORD
COMMISSIONER

HURLEY W. RUDD
COMMISSIONER

RICHARD P. "DICK" WILSON
COMMISSIONER

DANIEL A. KLEMAN
CITY MANAGER

HERBERT J. SECKEL
CITY AUDITOR-CLERK

BRYAN W. HENRY
CITY ATTORNEY

TELEPHONE
(904) 599-8100

CITY HALL
32304

September 28, 1978

Mr. William Earl Levy, Sr.
City of Tallahassee
Tallahassee, Florida

Dear Earl:

    On this day, Thursday, September 28, 1978, at 2:30 p.m. at the unveiling of the plaque commemorating the William Earl Levy, Sr. Fire Headquarters Building, I am hereby appointing you as the official lifetime Honorary Fire Chief of Tallahassee, Florida.

Warm personal regards,

Daniel A. Kleman
City Manager

DAK/vs

Appendix E

Miscellaneous Documents

- Training Syllabus

- Chief Levy on Fire Prevention December 8, 1945 – *Tallahassee Democrat*

- City publication *Panarama of Progress* – April, 1966

- "Good Government" newspaper article – *Tallahassee Democrat*

- "How to Protect You from Fire" *Memphis Press-Scimitar* February 21, 1957

- Letter from Chief Levy to Mrs. J. Kittrell on the history of the old fire bell – February 27, 1975

IN-SERVICE TRAINING
TALLAHASSEE, FLORIDA, FIRE DEPARTMENT

Because the nature of Fire Department training is quite different from most in-service training programs, we take the liberty of summarizing our program herein rather than use the questionaire supplied, which in our opinion, is not appropriate for our use.

When a person has been employed, we refer to him as an inductee. He serves a probationary period of one year, during which time he receives basic courses in firemanship. He then serves an additional three years during which time he progresses to first class firefighter.

Regardless of the years of service, or the rank attained, each individual takes refresher courses, courses embracing new allied subjects, etc.

Course frequency is difficult to establish, but some type of instruction dealing with one or more varying subjects is being given almost daily.

The department has a full-time Training officer, whose duty is to prepare course outlines, class schedules, etc., under the direction of the Chief of Department. He teaches classes in special related subjects and supervises "company drill." (This is where a group of men who work together as a unit, perform in order to put what they have learned into practice and become, or remain, proficient.)

The company officers may give certain classes, in each fire station, to the men under their direct supervision, in planned 2-hour sessions.

The department has a training center which includes classroom facilities, training officer's office, drill tower, paved drill area, etc. This facility is used for all appropriate training.

Most class periods are two hours in length, and of course all personnel are required to satisfactorily complete the courses given. Examinations are given and a passing grade of 70% is required.

The courses are available to Tallahassee Fire Department personnel only except by special arrangement with the Chief of Department. The faculty is as given above, but occasionally outside experts in allied subject material may be obtained, such as people from the Atomic Energy Commission, Civil Defense etc.

For special training, the training officer, fire prevention officer, and others quite often attend schools at such locations as the Florida Fire College, University of Maryland, etc. as well as often attending seminars, workshops, and others.

Each of the courses listed below is designed to be thirty hours each. The first six are basic courses and the others are for continuing education. An example of the amount of content in these is the fact that the first six courses utilize over 60 instructional guide sheets.

       Forcible Entry, Rope and Extinguisher Practices
       Ladder Practices
       Hose Practices
       Salvage and Overhaul Practices
       Fire Stream Practices
       Apparatus Practices
       Ventilation Practices

Rescue Practices
  First Aid Practices
  Inspection Practices

Officer training courses embrace the following subjects:

  Fire Department Organization
  Fire Company Supervision
  Fire Department Administration
  Non Fire Fighting Functions
  Public and Human Relations
  Water Supplies

Examples of courses embracing related information are:

  Peacetime Radiation Hazards
  Communications
  Driver Training, etc.

In a resume' such as this, it is impossible to properly convey the depth of the program, but a closing example of its extent is the fact that during a one-year period ending September 30, 1965, more than 2,400 manhours of supervised training was given.

Attached, you will find a typical sample copy of a special text on Principles of Resuscitation. (This is related information about principles and use of a special piece of equipment, the E & J Resuscitator.) And also a copy of the Instructors Guide Sheet for the same course. This guide sheet is prepared so that each company officer can give instruction to his men.

LEVY ISSUES WARNING

Fire Prevention For Homes Are

In a move to cut down losses caused by fires, Fire Chief Earl Levy last night warned residents here to take all possible precautions in heating their establishments and pointed out that most fires have been caused during the winter months by defective heating arangements.

"The most frequent cause of fires," he explained, "is the practice of lighting certain portable oil heating units and then failing to regulate them immediately. Unless properly regulated, the burner will overflow with flaming oil and spread, thereby causing a dangerous fire."

Another factor which frequently causes fires, he said, is the placing of wooden or cardboard fuel containers too close to the heating unit.

Placing of circulating heaters too close to walls and in narrow halls also comes in for a share of the blame in causing fires, Levy said. "When radiating heaters were in use more than they are now, there wasn't so much danger because they usually were placed in the center of a room, but now with circulating heaters so popular, people tend to have them placed too close to the wall believing, no doubt, that the outer metal covering is sufficient protection.

"It does provide some protection but if placed too close to the wall it is no protection at all."

Levy blamed faulty electrical wiring for causing many fires. But he explained that residents would have fewer fires from this cause if they would refrain from placing copper coins in the end of a blown out fuse.

Whenever a fuse blows out, that is a danger signal that the electrical wiring or some electrical appliance is faulty. Instead of just replacing the fuse and forgetting it blew out, a person should ask some qualified electrician to locate the cause of the trouble.

Levy suggested seven measures as safety precautions:

"Check furnaces and stoves carefully for worn, broken or rusted parts, and repair or replace when necessary. Also remove soot.

"Replace rusty smokepipes and those having holes through which hot sparks could fly.

"Look for burnable materials that have become blackened from radiated heat and may catch fire. A clearance of 18 inches usually is required all around and above heating plants. If necessary, burnable material may be protected with metal and sheet asbestos insulation, leaving an airspace of one inch between the insulation and the material.

"Inspect chimneys for cracks and loose mortar and have them repaired where necessary. Remove soot. All chimneys should have flue linings of fire clay.

"Never 'force' the furnace if you don't get enough warmth, as the equipment may overheat. Call in a heating engineer, who may be able to make the plant function more efficiently and economically.

"When banking a fire, leave some uncovered hot coals at the front to ignite coal gas.

"Empty hot ashes into metal containers — never wood boxes or cartons."

As a last precaution, Chief Levy recommended that every resident should decide what exit he would use in case of fire in any part of the house. He suggested that persons who live on upper floors of residences and apartment houses should pay especial attention to ways of quick exit.

PANARAMA of PROGRESS

Vol. 1, No. 4
April, 1966

CITY OF TALLAHASSEE, FLORIDA
FLORIDA'S CAPITAL CITY—SERVING ALL FLORIDA

FIRE DEPT. HAS GOOD YEAR IN '65

TRAINING AND FIRE PREVENTION PAYS

The successful 1965 year for the Tallahassee Fire Department has been credited to a continuing fire prevention program and training activities for the department.

The 1965 annual report reveals department personnel devoted over 1,400 hours to training activities during the year. Most of these hours were devoted to nine different training programs; aerial ladder, radiation hazards in the fire service, fire fighting tactics, apparatus practices, pumper hookup to hydrants, apparatus practice related to familiarization with new equipment, emergency power system operation, driver training for aerial ladder truck, driver training for combined operation of pumper and tanker.

Constant training in the above areas helped maintain the department at peak efficiency with the successful suppression of fires a direct result.

The other half of the program — fire prevention — includes a variety of activities from fire prevention programs to building inspections and investigations. Levy's report cites the contributions of various segments of the community as being responsible for the success of the fire prevention activities. He said many organizations, individuals and mass communications media are responsible for producing the present desirable situation.

Fire department personnel completed over 400 building inspections as a part of their 1965 fire prevention activities — this included 314 commercial buildings, 62 automatic sprinkler systems, and 31 homes. They also provided 26 fire prevention talks or programs to different groups. Thirty-two special investigations of fires were also completed.

> **YIELD THE RIGHT-OF-WAY TO FIRE DEPARTMENT EMERGENCY VEHICLES**

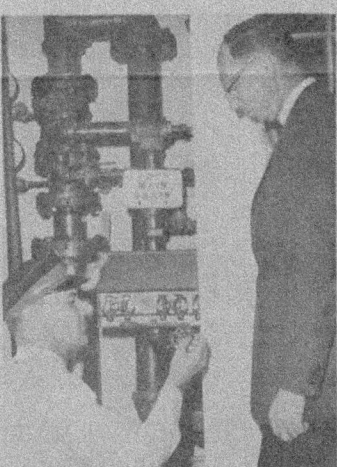

CAPT. JAMES CURETON of the Tallahassee Fire Department and Bill Watson, safety coordinator at FSU check the sprinkler system in one of the dormitories at the university. The Fire Department maintains a regular inspection schedule of the university buildings.

TALLAHASSEE'S FIRE RATING GOOD

As a result of the outstanding effectiveness of the Tallahassee Fire Department over the years, Tallahassee has a rank three classification for fire insurance purposes. Cities are classed from one to ten by fire insurance underwriters for insurance rates. Class one is the highest or best classification and class 10 is the lowest or highest fire loss classification.

Tallahassee is one of only about six Florida cities having a class three rating. This class three rating results in Tallahassee residents paying lower insurance rates than people in most of the other cities in the nation.

LEVY SUBMITS ANNUAL REPORT

Tallahassee's per capita fire loss for 1965 was only $2.50. This is a decrease from $11.63 per capita in 1960.

LEVY

The annual report of the Tallahassee Fire Department submitted by Chief Earl Levy to City Manager Arvah Hopkins reveals the total fire loss in the City of Tallahassee has dropped from $569,825.56 in 1960 to $154,743.51 in the past year. The city's population during this same period has risen from 49,000 to an estimated 63,000.

The decrease in per capita fire loss and total fire loss has been brought about, in part, according to the report by an effective fire prevention campaign over the years and intensive training activities conducted by the fire department personnel. Levy gives credit in his report to the various segments of the public including the mass communications media for the success of the fire prevention activities.

During the 1965 year fire department personnel participated in nine different training activities and devoted a total of more than 1,400 hours to training. They concentrated in such areas as aerial ladder training, radiation hazards, fire fighting tactics, emergency power system operations, driver training and other related activities.

The department completed over 400 inspections of buildings, conducted 26 fire prevention programs and completed 32 special investigations of fires, according to the report.

> **TALLAHASSEE'S 1965 PER CAPITA FIRE LOSS $2.50**

CHIEF LEVY SERVES CAPITAL CITY 39 YEARS

Tallahassee Fire Chief Earl Levy has observed numerous changes in fire fighting in Tallahassee during his years of service with the Tallahassee Fire Department.

During his tenure with the fire department, he has watched the city grow and the fire department keep pace with that growth. When he began his public service career on March 15, 1927, the Tallahassee Fire Department was located at the central (and only) station on south Adams Street in the building located on the corner of Jefferson Street. This building also served as the City Hall.

In 1937 a new station was built on north Adams Street at the present location of the main fire station. Currently the fire department is housed in five different stations strategically located in different sections of the city. Instead of the nine men which made up the 1927 force, Levy supervises over 90 men.

It is quite likely Earl Levy has served as chief of a municipal fire department longer than any other fire chief currently serving any other major Florida city. He has a grand total of 39 years service and 26 years as chief. He was appointed chief of the Tallahassee Fire Department in May of 1940.

During his years of service, Levy has kept the fire department in step with current developments and as a result, the fire insurance rates have been lowered and the fire classification for the city has gone from a class six to an outstanding class three. In addition to providing leadership for the local department, Levy has played an outstanding role in professional firemen's activities, and has received many awards from different organizations for his devotion to public service.

Chief Levy is married to the former Hassell Williams of Savannah, Georgia. They have two sons, William Earl, Jr. and Frederick Cartwright Levy.

SUMMARY ANNUAL REPORT
1961-1965

Year	Population	Per Capita Loss	Fire Loss
1961	51,000	$1.83	$ 93,299.35
1962	51,500	3.12	162,175.36
1963	51,500	2.70	139,229.10
1964	58,000	2.31	133,905.90
1965	62,000	2.50	154,743.51

Year	National Per Capita	Tallahassee Per Capita
1961	$8.34	$1.83
1962	8.57	3.12
1963	9.46	2.70
1964	8.77	2.31
1965		2.50

TALLAHASSEE'S MISS FLAME VISITS FIRE DEPARTMENT — Miss Janice Dutcher, a sophomore at Florida State University selected as 1965 Miss Flame by the Tallahassee Jaycees recently paid a visit to the Tallahassee Fire Department. She is seen (l to r) trying on a fireman's jacket, (inspecting the traffic control device at the Main Fire Station) and trying out the tillerman's seat on the 100' ladder truck.

MISS FLAME VISITS FIRE DEPARTMENT

PANARAMA OF PROGRESS is published monthly by the Public Relations Department of the City of Tallahassee, Florida. Huey B. Long is editor and offices are located in City Hall. PANARAMA OF PROGRESS is dedicated to informing the citizens and residents of the City of Tallahassee of city projects which affect their daily lives. Extra copies may be obtained upon request.

CITY OF TALLAHASSEE, FLA.
CITY HALL

BULK RATE
U. S. POSTAGE
PAID
Tallahassee, Fla.
Permit No. 1

FIRE CHIEF Earl Levy, right, is being congratulated by Jaycee awards committee chairman Rufus Jefferson, for his outstanding public service.

He Cuts Down Fire Losses
Fire Chief Levy Wins Good Government Award

Tallahassee Fire Chief Earl Levy was winner last night of the Jaycee Good Government Award, given annually to an official whose diligence goes beyond his ordinary responsibility.

Rufus Jefferson, chairman of the selection committee, made the presentation before 155 Jaycees and their guests during the annual banquet at the Floridan Hotel.

Mr. Jefferson characterized Chief Levy's operation of his office as being so "efficient it threatens to put the insurance people out of business."

He revealed that during Chief Levy's tenure of office the fire rate has dropped yearly until Tallahassee now ranks with cities having the lowest incidence of fire per capita in the United States.

The fire chief was also praised for his "countless" speeches before (Continued on Page 2)

various groups in behalf of fire prevention and safety.

Al Thomasson, Jaycee publicity director, was awarded the Certificate of Merit for outstanding work in that post.

Installation of new club officers by State President Charles Johnson of Jacksonville was another highlight of the evening.

Taking office were Roy Rhodes as president, Fred Drake, first vice president, and Bob Grennberg, second vice president.

Jerry Thomas was master of ceremonies. Miss Delano Driver, Miss Tallahassee of 1955, was a guest vocalist.

The evening was concluded with a dance in the hotel ballroom.

Memphis Press-Scimitar

SECOND SECTION—PA

FIRE INSTRUCTORS PANEL—Opening day speakers at the Fire Department Instructors Conference are shown above with Memphis Fire Chief John C. Klinck, center. Left to right are Fire Chief Earl Levy of Tallahassee, Fla.; Robert C. Byrus, of the University of Maryland; Chief Klinck; Chief Albert H. Petersen of Chicago and Chief O. E. Hirst of Galena, Ill.

Eight Were Defia Why Did Congres Cite Only Four?

Perkins Explains Differenc In Union Men's Positions

By FRED W. PERKINS, Scripps-Howard Staff

WASHINGTON.—Lawyers noted with inte that the Senate yesterday unanimously cited tempt of Congress only four of eight witnesse refused to answer questions from the Senate tions Committee probing rackets in labor uni

Legal theories revolved around two circums

1. The cited quartet—two major and t officers of the Teamsters Union—all based fusals on a questio committee's authorit gate in the labor fiel

2. The others—all in the Teamster or pleaded and insisted constitutional rights Fifth Amendment, tects individuals fr crimination.

Lawyer Explains

The difference betw defenses has been ou Federal Bar Journal Hitz, assistant U. S. the District of Colum conducted most of t tions in recent years of contempt of Congr refusals to answer.

Since 1858, nearly ago, when the first of this sort was ins prosecutions have b in the District of C this charge. There a few in other jurisdic the actual offense wa have occurred.

Hitz wrote:

"There has not be sustained conviction c of Congress by a w refused to answer up of privilege against a nation where the pri actually claimed an waived by the witnes

Some Exceptions

However, he noted, witnesses ran afoul and were convicted b courts found they di tively claim the privil waived it by partial di

How to Protect You From Fire

It's Topic for 2000 Gathered in City

By LILLIAN FOSCUE
Press-Scimitar Staff Writer

How to better protect the lives and property of the nation from fire is the common aim of more than 2000 men gathered in Memphis this week.

Representatives of fire departments thruout the country and Canada opened the 29th annual Fire Department Instructors Conference at the Auditorium.

"Fire protection in nursing homes is a problem we need to look on," Robert C. Byrus of the University of Maryland pointed out.

"If any place should have adequate protection, it should be a nursing home where the majority of residents are not able to get themselves out in the event of fire," Byrus said.

Byrus said the two recent public nursing home fires, one in Missouri, the other in Iowa, has brought the problem to public consciousness tho fire fighters have been aware of the danger for a number of years.

Byrus said universities are lagging in the fire protection pro.

1. The University of Maryland has added a degree in fire protection engineering only this Oklahoma A&M and Illinois Institute already offered a degree.

rus and Fire Chief Albert H. sen of Chicago commended phis on its fire prevention am, which includes housese inspections.

Chicago," Petersen said.

A 'Has-Been' at 35—Diana Tells How It Happened

Life Story of Barrymore's Daughter Begins—It Pulls No Punches

By United Press

NEW YORK.—Diana Barrymore had her first drink at 13. Her father ordered it for her at a restaurant because he thought Barrymores should get an early start.

Beginning her life story in the current issue of Look Magazine, the 35-year-old actress describes herself as a "has-been"—a girl who had everything and "seems to have tried hard to throw it all away."

Born to actor John Barrymore and poet Michael Strange (Blanche Oelrichs of Newport society), Miss Barrymore recalls that she was brought up by servants. Her mother was too busy with writing and society, and her father was off wooing his leading lady, Dolores Costello.

She didn't meet her father until she was eight years old. He breezed into the home of her new stepfather, New York attorney Harrison Tweed, and told her "you really look like your Aunt Ethel," and was gone. The next time she saw him was when she was 13 and a student at a Baltimore finishing school.

"We found ourselves in a luxurious restaurant," Miss Barrymore wrote. "Daddy turned to me. 'Treepee,' he said doubtfully, 'would you like something to begin with'?"

When she told him she'd never had a cocktail, Barrymore mused that she "certainly didn't sound like a Barrymore"—or an Oelrichs, either. He ordered her a Brandy Alexander, explaining that it was "exactly like a milk shake." She had two. Her father passed out before he got her back to school.

Miss Barrymore said she had

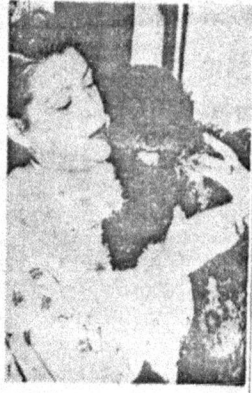

MISS BARRYMORE and her black poodle.

Here He Comes, There He Goes

Back and Forth He Went in Hot Cars

By Associated Press

GREENVILLE, Miss.

Satchmo's Band Is Target Of Dynamiting

Miss Single Beat But Combo Doesn't

By UNITED PRESS

Louis Armstrong, the negro trumpet player whose concert was targeted by a dynamiting last night in Knoxville, Tenn., said the demonstration will not hamper his Southern tour.

"I've been playing the horns for 44 years an never had any trouble before," Satchmo said, commenting on the blast set off outside the auditorium in city-owned Chilhowee Park.

Armstrong was bearing down on his "Back o' Town Blues" when two or three sticks of dynamite exploded outside, sending a shock wave thru the segregated auditorium jammed with 2000 white and 1000 negro jazz fans.

There was a stir. Many heads turned toward the direction of the earth-shaking explosion, which tore a five-foot hole in the ground outside. But it did no other damage and no one was hurt.

'My Phone Ringing'

EARL L. YANCEY
MAYOR-COMMISSIONER

JOHN R. JONES
MAYOR PRO TEM-COMMISSIONER

JAMES R. FORD
COMMISSIONER

JOAN R. HEGGEN
COMMISSIONER

DONALD C. PRICE
COMMISSIONER

DANIEL A. KLEMAN
CITY MANAGER

HERBERT J. SECKEL
CITY AUDITOR-CLERK

BRYAN W. HENRY
CITY ATTORNEY

EDW. J. HILL
CITY SOLICITOR

February 27, 1975

Mrs. Joe B. Kittrell
317 Mill Branch Road
Tallahassee, Florida

Dear Mrs. Kittrell:

First, let me apologize profoundly to you for being so late in replying to your letter about the old fire bell.

The history of the bell dates far back. It was installed in the tower of the old city hall building at the southeast corner of Adams and Jefferson streets and was rung in connection with a system of coded signals based on the number of strikes. The area within the city limits was divided into a number of physical sections divided by specified street boundaries on all four sides.

In the terminology used by the volunteer firemen at that time those areas were known as districts. The term "district" as was used then was in no sense the same as the same term today which implies a special tax district for fire protection. The fire department in those days was supported entirely as it is today by the municipality.

These districts were numbered typically in such fashion as 12, 13, 14, in multiples of 20's and 30's and so forth.

When an alarm was turned in by a phone call to the station, a certain metal disc with the required number was set in such fashion that it would activate the bell to ring the numbers in series, as for instance "25" would be two rings with a 20 or 30 second delay then five consecutive rings. This would be repeated automatically 4 or 5 times with proper intervals between.

The volunteers could easily hear this bell all over the city which was quite small in those days. As I recall it, the bell must have been discontinued back in the 1930's. Since the original Tallahassee Volunteer Fire Department was organized around the year 1903, it is my feeling

"FLORIDA'S CAPITAL CITY" — SERVING ALL FLORIDA

Page 2 - Mrs. Kittrell - February 27, 1975

that the bell must have been installed sometime before 1910.

It was used for all the years thereafter consistently from about the time mentioned above. I have very fond personal recollections of hearing it ring, and I have personally set the discs in place to ring the various districts on many occasions during the '30's.

It was quite a thing to hear this bell at three or four o'clock in the morning, and the sounds seemed to create a feeling of great urgency. I am personally very glad to know the church expects to keep this bell permanently for we in the fire department feel quite sentimental about it.

I might explain to you further that the bell was in a rigid position in such a fashion that a metal hammer which was rigidly attached to a shaft actually did the striking. The shaft was activated by a 1,000 pound weight of iron discs hung on a cable which was automated an inch or two at a time by the gravitational weight of this 1,000 pounds of iron fastened to the cable. The mechanism was activated electrically by a set of storage batteries which provided current to the street fire alarm box system also. The dropping of the weights was governed by electrical impulses which were controlled by the discs we mentioned before.

I trust this information will be of help to you.

Sincerely,

Earl Levy
Chief, Fire Department
327 North Adams Street
Tallahassee, Florida

el:mj

About the Author

Maurice Majszak is retired from the U.S. Navy (Chief Warrant Officer), City of Miami Fire Department, City of Miramar Fire-Rescue (Fire Marshal) and City of Tallahassee Fire Department. He is certified as Fire Instructor III, Fire Inspector I, Fire Inspector II, and Fire Investigator I in the State of Florida. Maurice was the Broward County Fire Inspector of the Year in 2003 and Florida Fire Inspector of the Year in 2008. He has been an Adjunct Instructor at Broward Community College, Broward County, FL and the National Fire Academy in Emmitsburg, MD. He has served on the Florida Fire Marshal's and Inspector Association Legislative Committee and on the State-wide Informal Fire Code Interpretation Committee.

He currently lives in Tallahassee with his wife, Jo Ellen. They have four children, Sherri, Doug, Cindi and Mark. Maurice is active in preserving Tallahassee Fire Department history. He is author of the book "Remembering the Tallahassee Fire Department" and the unofficial Fire Department Historian. With too many degrees to list, Maurice has been instrumental in establishing the Hydrant Garden in front of Tallahassee Fire Station 1 at 327 N. Adams Street, and the Tallahassee Fire Department Museum. Maurice is a member of the Florida State Firefighters Association, Florida Fire Marshals and Inspectors Association, National Fire Academy Alumni Association, and Florida Antique Bucket Brigade

INDEX

Albertson
    Carol 35
Arnold
    Bill 63
Avon Park Fire Department vii
Barineau
    Hantz 49
Barnett
    Bill 45
Barron
    Dempsey 52
Beville
    E.F. 31
Byrd
    Jimmy 25
Calloway
    Jimmy 17
Carnegie
    Dale 47
Carter
    Robert W. 32
Coe
    Ridgeway .... vii, 19, 28, 37
    Ridgway 22
    T.P. 5, 19, 31, 44
    Thomas Pinkney (TP) 1
Collins
    Leroy 2
Culley & Sons Guardian Funeral
    Home Chapel 55
Culpepper Jr.
    Horrie 28
Cureton
    James 39
Dale Mabry Air Field 54
David Walker Library 22
Deal
    Charlie 13, 46
Elberta Crate Factory 34
Everhart
    Lee A. 49
First Baptist Church 6, 55
First National Bank 5
Florida A&M 34
Florida Fireman .... vii, 31
Florida State Fire College 41
Florida State Firemen Association 31
Flowers
    Mack vii
Fountain
    Jeanette 35, 80
    Jeanette Levy .... vii, 11
FSU 34
Fuqua
    Don 53, 101
Gray
    R.A. 45
Guedry
    Bernard 35
Haney
    Tom 31
Hart
    B.B. 31
Heisler
    W. Fred 45
Hershey
    R.N. 31
Hopkins
    Arvah 35
    Arvah B. 51
Horne
    Mallory 51

Insurance Service Office (ISO) 26
Ireland
    Ken 52
ISO Classification 85
Jaws of Life 28
Jefferson
    Rufus 46
Johnson
    Clyde 39
Jones
    Melba 5, 43, 69
Kinard
    W.O. 21
Kittrell
    Mrs. Joe 38
Kleman
    Dan 17, 43
Knight
    William Thomas 50
Knowles
    Mike .... vii, 28
Lake Jackson 8
Larson
    J. Edwin 48
Lee
    Clyde 35
Leon Federal Credit Union 21
Leon High School 3
Levy
    Bessie 1
    Bill .... vii, 3, 8
    Fred 1, 2
    Hassell 13
    Hassell Williams 4
    Jeanette 1, 31
    Myrtle 1
    O'Neal 1
    Rick .... viii, 8, 10, 73, 77
    William Earl i
Lewis Sr.
    George E. 49
Love
    Raymond 25
McDaniel
    George 11
McIver
    John 80
Mendelson's Department Store ... 21, 22
Middlebrooks
    Mr. 7
Mitchell
    Fred 40
Newport 9
Oakland Cemetery 5, 55
Old Plank Road 9
Palmer
    Henry 49
Panarama of Progress 33
Pfhaender
    F.C. 31
Proctor
    Ralph 49
    Theo 49
Proctor, Sr
    Ralph E. 52
Pumphrey
    Don 14
Ragsdale
    Burr 49
Raines
    Guy 27, 29
Revell Jr.
    Reese 44
Roberts
    Herb 36
    Tommy 29

Robertson
- James C. 43
- Robbie .... vii, 17, 30, 32

Roselawn Cemetery 40

Sadler
- A.P. 31

Savage
- John J. 50

Sexton
- Tom 45

Smith
- Rutledge 31

St. Marks River 10

Stoutamire
- Sidney 29

Sullivan
- Kate 3

Surles
- Larry .... viii, 16, 70

Swearingen
- James 29

Tacot Stables 8

Tallahassee Gazette 18, 41

Tallahassee Volunteer Fire Company 3

Thomas
- Pat 52

Townsend
- C.P. 31

Trot-a-Way Club 8

Vinzant
- Joe 24

Wahnish
- Sam 49

Wainwright
- Morris 11, 39, 42

Walker
- May 37

Warren
- Fuller 45

Washington Hall Hotel 21

Williams
- Broward 48

Wynn
- Ed 35, 40

Yeager Sr.
- Jack 49

Leon County, Florida Heritage Book; Historical Stories of Events, Places & People that Shaped Tallahassee

More Tallahassee History

This delightful book is a compilation of stories depicting the history of Leon County. The stories were written and submitted by different authors and families. The text includes a wide variety of topics and time periods ranging from the 1820s to modern day. Many of the stories contain photos that were submitted by the author. The subject matter is divided into several categories that include;
LEON COUNTY ARTS & ENTERTAINMENT
LEON COUNTY BUSINESSES
LEON COUNTY COMMUNITIES
LEON COUNTY SCHOOLS AND UNIVERSITIES
LEON COUNTY LOCAL LANDMARKS
LEON COUNTY ORGANIZATIONS
RELIGIOUS COMMUNITIES/CEMETERIES
LEON COUNTY SPECIAL EVENTS
LEON COUNTY REMINISCENCES
LEON COUNTY FAMILIES

The Tallahassee Genealogical Society, Inc. has compiled a book that represents many of the threads that over time have been woven into the community of Leon County. Overall, this book is an intriguing mixture of the old, the new, the events, the places & the people that shaped Tallahassee.

Shop Now: www.syppublishing.com

www.ingramcontent.com/pod-product-compliance
Lightning Source LLC
Chambersburg PA
CBHW080547170426
43195CB00016B/2709